brilliant

confidence

confidence

How to challenge your fears and go for anything you want in life

Mike McClement

Prentice Hall
is an imprint of

Harlow, England • London • New York • Boston • San Francisco • Toronto • Sydney • Singapore • Hong Kong
Tokyo • Seoul • Taipei • New Delhi • Cape Town • Madrid • Mexico City • Amsterdam • Munich • Paris • Milan

PEARSON EDUCATION LIMITED

Edinburgh Gate
Harlow CM20 2JE
Tel: +44 (0)1279 623623
Fax: +44 (0)1279 431059
Website: www.pearsoned.co.uk

First published in Great Britain in 2010

Pearson Education is not responsible for the content of third party internet sites.

ISBN: 978-0-273-73588-5

British Library Cataloguing-in-Publication Data
A catalog record for this book is available from the British Library

Library of Congress Cataloging-in-Publication Data
McClement, Mike.
Brilliant confidence : how to challenge your fears and go for anything you want in life / Mike McClement
        p. cm.
    ISBN 978-0-273-735885 (pbk.)
    1. Self-confidence. 2. Self-esteem. 3. Confidence. I. Title.
    BF575.S39M33 2010
    158.--dc22

                                                        2010023717

10 9 8 7 6 5 4 3 2 1
13 12 11 10 09

Typeset in 10/14pt Plantin by 3
Printed and bound in Great Britain by Henry Ling Ltd, Dorchester, Dorset

Contents

About the author

Mike McClement has 20 years' experience in the field of personal development.

He founded *Training Hand Ltd* in 1995 and, more recently, its sister company *Think Confidence*. Both companies focus on the provision of personal development training and coaching.

Mike's professional expertise is in the areas of self-confidence, assertiveness, motivation and personal effectiveness. His work centres around the development and facilitation of bespoke training for groups and, on a more personal level, one-to-one coaching programmes for individuals. He also delivers speeches and short workshops on confidence and motivation at business events and conferences.

In business, he works in both the public and private sectors and at all levels of seniority; from chief executive to junior staff member. His courses are also popular with people who need to build their confidence in their personal lives outside work. His particular interest and motivation lies in the challenge of helping people to realise their full potential.

Mike lives in Devon with his wife and three young children.

Email: mike@thinkconfidence.com

 Join Mike on Linkedin

Follow Mike on twitter http://twitter.com/thinkconfidence

Find Mike's blog at http://blog.thinkconfidence.com

Join Think Confidence on Facebook

Acknowledgements

My thanks go to everyone who has helped me in the writing of the book. In particular, my wife, Jenny, for all the support she's given and for her hard work and expertise in creating the www.thinkconfidence.com website. Thank you also to my children, Madeleine, Toby and Anna, for having so much patience throughout the project. My thanks also go to James Crooke from www.cj-design.com for creating the software for the Think Confidence Reality Check.

Lastly, thank you to all the people whose experiences are mentioned in the book. Although their names have been changed, it would not have been possible to write the book without reference to real people who have struggled with confidence and succeeded in overcoming their difficulties. I thank them all and wish them luck for the future.

Introduction

It took Sid 18 months to build his house. I watched him from my window every day, right from the start to the finish. He didn't rush, he didn't cut corners, he took one step at a time, he had a plan; he knew what he wanted his house to look like. Mostly he worked alone, just occasionally he needed help. At the end he stood there looking up, in front of his new house. I remember that day well; I watched him open the front door and walk proudly in.

Brick by brick, Sid had built his house.

This is a true story about a neighbour of mine who demolished an old farm building and built a house in its place. I think about him every now and then. He started with nothing but wasn't daunted by the task ahead. He knew the size of his challenge but he didn't let it frighten him. I got to know him well while he was building. I found it fascinating watching his progress. I was amazed when he told me it was the first time he'd ever built a house!

You too have a challenge ahead; think of it as your 'Confidence Project'. My neighbour built his house; you're going to build your confidence. Sid is a great role model. You'll need to take the same approach as he did. It might not take you 18 months but it's not going to happen overnight.

Don't worry. I'm not trying to frighten you off! I'm just preparing you for the challenge ahead. It'll be incredibly rewarding if you commit to it. You'll need self-discipline, courage and energy. At times you'll feel frustrated and at other times you'll feel emotional. Don't give up, never give up; keep persevering and, step by step, your confidence, self-belief and self-esteem will grow.

Think back over the last few weeks and months. How many times have you lacked the self-confidence to do something you *know* you should have done? Something that would have helped you; something that was right for you; something, perhaps, that you would have enjoyed? Or how many times have you not spoken up when you knew you were right?

If you're honest with yourself, the answer to these questions will probably be 'quite a few'. That's because very few people have the self-confidence, self-belief and self-discipline to do the right thing all the time. Imagine how *you'd* feel if you could confidently answer 'Never' to these questions. Well, it can happen, everyone can do it.

Brilliant Confidence is a practical and logical no-nonsense solution to this. It relates directly to the reality of life. It can be applied to both your work life and your social life. It's full of practical advice and examples of how real people have overcome their lack of confidence or self-esteem; real people who have made real changes to their lives.

> you'll learn things about yourself that you didn't know, things perhaps that you didn't think were important

Get ready though; the book will challenge you. It will invite you to reflect and it will make you think. You'll learn things about yourself that you didn't know, things perhaps that you didn't think were important.

The book is linked to the www.thinkconfidence.com website. Here you'll find links to other reading material. There are also questionnaires you can complete to learn more about yourself and your confidence levels in relation to the way you communicate and deal with conflict. You can even take the Think Confidence Reality Check, which invites others to give you feedback on *their* perception of you in terms of your confidence, communication style and assertiveness.

In short, by using the techniques addressed in the book, you'll develop the self-confidence to overcome your fears, seize opportunities, speak up when required, enjoy yourself and live life to the full.

PART 1

Creating the confident mindset

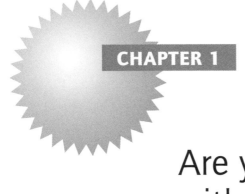

CHAPTER 1

Are you born with self-confidence?

I lost count a long time ago of the number of people who ask me the question 'Surely you're born with self-confidence?' They're convinced that some people are just lucky because they're 'born' confident. This just isn't true.

The first thing to accept about confidence is that at birth we are all on a level playing field. We all start together at the same point on the path to self-confidence. If you continue to think you're at a disadvantage to confident people because you weren't born confident, then the playing field that used to be level will turn into a steeper and steeper upward climb.

So, before you read on, it's important to come to terms with this and *believe* it. Confident people aren't *born* confident. Confidence is an attitude that develops. It might be worth taking a few seconds to mull this over. Some people accept it but don't really believe it. If you don't believe it, it will become a convenient excuse. It then becomes a heavy burden that hinders you whenever you find yourself outside your comfort zone.

confident people aren't *born* confident

Now think of confidence as a *skill* that relates to your attitude and your state of mind. It isn't something concrete or something of substance that you can touch or put your finger on, but it is tangible. Controlling your state of mind, thinking positively and feeling that you can change for the better is one of the first steps on the road to increased self-confidence.

Remember you can acquire self-confidence at any stage in your life. You can *learn* how to feel and look more confident as you grow and mature. Everyone can do this. We all have the opportunity to build our self-confidence as our lives move on. *The key is to treat confidence as a skill.* You really *can* learn how to become more confident. Think back to other skills you have learnt as your life has moved on, for example reading, writing, riding a bike, or driving a car, and treat confidence in the same way.

brilliant tip

No one is born with confidence; it is a skill which we can all learn.

Why do you want to be more confident?

So let's get straight to the point. Why are you reading *Brilliant Confidence*? You'll have your own reasons. Some people are faced with a specific hurdle in their lives which they can't overcome due to their lack of self-confidence. Others are struggling with a number of issues relating to confidence, self-belief or self-esteem. Or perhaps you're one of the people who doesn't feel they have any major issues to address but simply sees confidence as an essential 'life-skill' that successful people learn.

Whatever your reasons, if you answer 'Yes' to any of the following questions, *Brilliant Confidence* will focus your mind and present solutions.

Would you like to be able to:

Yes / No

- Seize opportunities before they pass you by?   ☐ ☐
- Speak up when you know you're right?   ☐ ☐

Yes / No

- Feel comfortable and in control straight away when
  you walk into a room of people you don't know?   ☐ ☐

- Be more assertive and influential so that people fully
  understand what you need and your point of view?   ☐ ☐

- Overcome and use to positive effect the nerves you
  might feel when speaking in public?   ☐ ☐

- Present your thoughts clearly and confidently even
  when you fear the person may disagree with you?   ☐ ☐

- Introduce yourself confidently and charismatically at
  social events and work meetings?   ☐ ☐

- Wake up every morning and feel motivated and clear
  about what you aim to achieve from the day ahead,
  both at work and in your personal life?   ☐ ☐

- Boost your self-esteem and overcome any negative
  perceptions that are holding you back?   ☐ ☐

This list may look pretty daunting. Having read it, perhaps you're thinking to yourself: 'I can't be ... because I am not ...' or 'I couldn't possible behave like ... because I don't have ...' Well, let me straight away dispel a number of myths that exist about confidence. This will help to wipe the slate clean before we move on, and will clear up any misconceptions you may have.

The myths about self-confidence

Myth – You have to be talented to be confident

It's true that some people are naturally more talented at some things than others. For example, it's a fact that some people are naturally more gifted at sport than other people. It's also a fact that some people are gifted with high intelligence or perhaps the ability to sing well. So, there are indeed natural talents that we are born with. However, it doesn't automatically follow that you're going to be a naturally confident person.

There are some people who seem to exude confidence naturally. Think of people you see on television – people who perform to an audience of millions of people. This would seem an absolutely impossible task to the majority of us and you would probably think that someone who can perform in front of such large audiences couldn't possibly have problems with confidence. You'd be wrong. In a recent BBC news report, Robbie Williams was reported as having problems with confidence in his performance on *The X Factor*. The truth is that, no matter how talented you are, you can still suffer from a lack of confidence.

The key is to be satisfied in your own abilities and to know that you are giving your best. The way to make this work is to accept that what's important is what *you* think, not what others think about you.

brilliant tip

Don't worry if you think you lack talent. Try to harness the skills that you have. We all have strengths. It's what *you* think that matters, not what others think.

Myth – You have to be good looking or popular to be confident

You'll need to get this out of your mind. Your looks should not interfere with your confidence levels. Think about people you know who you would describe as confident. I'll bet the majority of them don't look like Brad Pitt or Angelina Joli, do they? In fact – would you describe *any* of them as good looking? Maybe one or two perhaps, but you'd expect that with the law of averages.

The key here is that it's not what you look like physically that's important. It's your self-belief and how you feel on the inside that forms the nucleus of self-confidence.

Think of Susan Boyle: she has been described as a 'hairy angel', an 'ugly duckling' and 'Shrek', Yet would you describe her as lacking in self-confidence? She is a great example of someone who is happy in her own skin and does not let her looks affect her approach to life.

brilliant tip

It doesn't matter what you look like. Your looks will have *no* impact on your confidence levels unless you let them.

Myth – Confidence is all about your physical presence

It's true that presenting yourself well helps if you want to come across confidently. However, you need more than just physical presence.

Physical presence and the assertive presentation of your thoughts is the last activity in a chain of events. To appear confident, every link in the chain needs to be strong. The strength of the chain and its ability to withstand stress is generated through your mindset. Having the strength of character to believe in yourself and your abilities is a critical element of the process.

Thinking positively is essential in relation to self-belief. We'll cover this and link it to ways you can develop and harness your self-belief in Chapter 2.

thinking positively is essential in relation to self-belief

brilliant tip

Physical presence has to be supported by self-belief in order to
generate self-confidence.

Myth – Confident people can deal with situations without even thinking about them

This just isn't true. Try asking a friend who you would describe
as confident – how it is that they manage to deal confidently with
situations they aren't expecting. If you don't have a confident
friend you know well enough, just watch how confident people
conduct themselves. You'll come up with the same answers
either way.

When dealing with an unexpected event, confident people
prepare properly before they act. They don't just jump in and
do or say something without thinking about it. In other words,
they have the self-discipline to create *time* for themselves.
Sometimes, all that's available is a few seconds – that's better
than nothing. Confident people have
the self-control to think about what
they are going to say before they say
it. There's pretty well always some
time available to do this. Confident
people create it and use it effectively.

> confident people have
> the self-control to think
> about what they are
> going to say before they
> say it

So, confident people don't have an in-built natural ability to deal
with situations off the cuff. They think before they act.

brilliant tip

Prepare properly before you commit. There's always time available. You
just need to have the presence of mind and confidence to grab it.

Myth – You need praise and appreciation from others to be confident

This isn't the case – and you should try not to let it be the case. It's nice to be appreciated and to be told you've done well or done a good job on occasions. However, it's not an essential requirement for self-confidence. It's true that some people need praise and appreciation more than others in order to feel confident. Even if you are one of these people, don't worry. If you work using personal achievement to motivate you, you'll feel less reliant on the praise and appreciation of others.

brilliant tip

Try to live and work for achievement, not praise and appreciation.

Changing your attitude and approach

Now that we've cast off a few myths, you should be in a stronger position to get started.

People lack confidence for many reasons. In fact I've never met two people who share the same reasons. It's quite often the case that someone's lack of confidence, self-esteem or self-belief originates from their experiences in life. Before we move on to consider how these experiences might have had an impact on you, it's helpful to reflect on how you approached life as a child.

Have you ever wondered why most young children have a natural instinct to learn? They seem to have an in-built curiosity about things they see and hear around them. In most cases, they're prepared to 'have a go' and try something out in order to satisfy this instinct. It's true that some children are naturally shy, but normally even they will eventually take a step forward and try something that interests them. Young children seem to have a natural self-belief and determination that drives a dynamo inside them. Parents will know that, on occasions, this dynamo can be so powerful that it's difficult to control!

So what's changed between then and now? Why does this dynamo that used to drive us now seem so slow? In some of us it may have even crusted up and jammed as time has moved on and we've matured. To start to feel and act more confidently, you need to get it working again.

This exercise will help to free up your dynamo.

---

brilliant exercise

Turning the clock back

Try to think back to when you were young. Think of a time when you learnt to do something that you've never forgotten since; something that has stayed with you right up to this point in your life. This might perhaps have been when you learnt to swim, to ride a bike or to do something else significant. Now think carefully about this experience and how, as a child, you approached it.

Write down some words or phrases that would help to describe your approach and how you remember feeling about that new challenge.

Don't read on just yet – complete the list of words or phrases first.

Now bring your mind back to more recent times, to the period of time over which you feel you've lacked self-confidence. Think of a situation that stands out; a situation that involved doing or learning something new; a situation when you remember your lack of confidence letting you down. This could be to do with work or your personal life – perhaps it was an interview you went to, a presentation you gave, a party you went to or maybe an argument you had with someone.

Now do the same as before and write down some words or phrases that would help to describe your approach and how you remember feeling about this more recent event.

When you've finished, look at the two lists together – reflect on the words you've chosen to describe the two experiences. Think first about the words you've written down to describe the experience when you were young. Ask yourself what they say about your approach to the task and what they tell you about your feelings.

You've probably written down words like 'fun', 'interesting', 'challenging', 'enjoyable', 'exciting' and phrases like 'no inhibitions', 'desperate to learn' and 'couldn't wait'. You've probably also written down words like 'anxious', 'difficult', 'scary', 'dangerous', 'embarrassing', 'sore', 'tiring', and 'frustrating' and phrases like 'didn't like it', 'couldn't do it at first' and 'found it really hard'.

How do these words and phrases differ from the ones you've used to describe your more recent experience? Ask yourself what the contrasts are. Is there a main theme you can draw out that encapsulates and describes your feelings and approach to each of the experiences?

Now identify and write down the main differences between the two lists. Does anything jump out at you? It shouldn't be long before you see how your approach to the challenge when you were young differs from your more recent experience. You can learn a great deal from this.

As a child, you had no inhibitions. As a child you wanted to learn new things and to tackle new challenges, even when these challenges were quite daunting. Trying new things was exciting as a child. You had a natural motivation and curiosity. You didn't fear failure, you probably didn't even think about failing. Your natural desire to learn just took over and propelled you on. You recognised the challenge and got on with achieving it with determination.

So, in essence, the list describing your childhood experience has a more positive, enthusiastic, focused and motivated feel to it. Yes, there are probably some negative words or phrases there but the key point is that you didn't let them get in the way. They didn't stop you striving to achieve the task.

If you could do this as a child, there's no reason why you can't do the same as an adult. There should be no reason why you can't learn new skills now, just as you did when you were young. The difficulty is that as we mature, other issues start to cloud our judgement. For example, we start to wonder what others might think, we start to worry about failing, we start to question our decisions, we start to look back at our other failures and, eventually, if we lack the confidence to take a step into the unknown, we decide that it would be safer to stay as we are. Or, depending on the situation, perhaps we decide that it would be safer not to say anything, not to rock the boat, not to risk upsetting someone.

So, reflect again now on the words you wrote down to describe your more recent experience. Think about why they tend to focus more on the negatives. Why are you letting them affect your approach and your confidence levels? Try telling yourself that nothing has changed since you were young – yes, you've grown up and matured physically but, in terms of your mindset, nothing has changed. So, therefore, there's no reason why you should behave any differently. Why are you letting those things that didn't bother you then bother you now?

brilliant tip

Don't let negative attitudes or pressures affect you. Try to approach new opportunities and challenges like you did as a child.

brilliant example

Sally

Sally lacked confidence. She was frustrated because she felt she was missing out on opportunities in her life. She had just moved to London and was living away from home for the first time. She was sharing a flat with an old friend from school. She wanted to make new friends and decided to take up ballroom dancing.

She did some research and found that a local hotel was organising ballroom dancing lessons on Thursday evenings. She persuaded her friend to go along too and they went for the first time. There were about 50 people there, none of whom they had met before. They spent the evening meeting new people and dancing with the guidance of an instructor, who stood on the stage and took the group through some simple moves.

Sally really enjoyed it and when they got home she told her friend she couldn't wait till next Thursday when they could go again for the next lesson. But her friend said she didn't really want to go again because she didn't enjoy it much. Sally was really disappointed and started to think twice about going again because she didn't want to go on her own.

Eventually, having thought about it all week, she summoned up the courage and went again the following Thursday. She hoped and prayed that some of the people she met last time would be there again so she didn't have to meet new people on her own. To her horror though, when she walked in, she didn't recognise a soul. She spent the evening feeling really uncomfortable and eventually decided to leave early. It just hadn't been the same without her friend – whereas before she'd found it easy to meet people, this time, without her friend there for support, she really struggled.

Sally found this incredibly frustrating because she knew she loved ballroom dancing and desperately wanted to carry on. Some weeks went by without her going. Then she decided to go on a confidence-building course in the hope that she might be able to overcome her fears. On the course, she was introduced to the concept of casting your mind back. In fact, her memories were very relevant because she thought back to the ballet lessons she had had when she was about six or seven years old. She remembered how much she'd enjoyed them and how she'd approached them. She reflected on her mental attitude back then as a child and how that might help her now. She realised that she needed to set aside her fears and her shyness.

The next week, she went again on the Thursday evening. On the way, she made a point of remembering how she'd found it so easy to relax into the ▶

situation when she was younger. With these memories at the forefront of her mind, she walked through the door at the start and thought positively about the whole experience. She forgot her inhibitions.

As a result she thoroughly enjoyed it. She hadn't known anyone when she walked in but had made four new dancing friends by the end.

---

brilliant tip

Think back to your attitude to learning new skills as a child. Try to set aside your inhibitions like you used to.

Learning from your experiences and those who influenced you

Childhood

So far, in relation to casting your mind back, we've talked in general terms about your attitude and how you can change it for the better by reflecting on how you used to approach new situations when you were young. Feelings like fear and anxiety just didn't exist then.

There are other lessons we can learn from thinking back. Have a look at these examples of people who've benefited by rewinding the clock back to their childhood. Do they ring any bells?

---

brilliant example

Miles

Miles, a 37-year-old accountant, was a shy person who had spent the majority of his adult life, in his words, 'lacking confidence and belief in myself'. I explained to him that it might help to reflect back on his experiences to see if he could remember any specific events that had affected his confidence levels. He tried this but couldn't remember anything in particular.

So I asked him about his childhood. Again, there was nothing he could remember about his childhood that stood out. In fact he described his childhood as 'normal, fun and loving'. Probing just a little, I asked him about his parents and how they brought him up. It was then that we started to make some progress – we established that both his parents were very shy people. Miles remembered them always trying to avoid meeting new people. In fact, he even remembered a specific situation when they went on holiday when he was about 11. They were staying in a hotel on one of the Greek islands. It was the first evening and everyone was invited down to the bar for the introductory talk by the holiday representative. Miles actually remembered his parents talking about the meeting and deciding not to go because it would mean 'meeting new people for the first time'.

Miles thought he'd forgotten about this because it was such a long time ago – but he hadn't. Not only had he not forgotten about it, but he now realised it had had quite an impact on him and his own confidence levels. He'd started to be like his parents. He had no idea, of course, that this was happening – why should he? After all, he respected his parents and thought this was just normal behaviour.

Miles found that reflecting constructively on his upbringing really helped. In fact the holiday meeting was just one example of many that he started to remember. He could see that his own approach to life had been radically affected by the behaviour and approach of both his parents.

This was a major turning point for him. He had identified the source of his lack of confidence. He knew that he now had to break the habit and felt motivated to get on with it.

So, when reflecting back on your childhood, open your mind as much as you can. You're not only trying to think back to experiences and challenges you were faced with. You're also reflecting on relationships you had, the culture in which you were brought up and the way people close to you approached their own lives.

brilliant example

Esther

Esther, a 42-year-old IT consultant, was beginning to feel that her life was being frittered away. She was happy in the sense that she was happily married and had two healthy teenage children. However, she was beginning to feel that 'life was beginning to pass me by' and that she was missing out on opportunities. This was really starting to frustrate her. She put this down to her lack of self-confidence because she found it hard to take the first step towards doing anything new or different.

Like Miles in the previous example, she reflected back on her life to see if she could identify anything that had happened to her that might explain this. She couldn't think of anything though. Then she started to think about how she had been brought up. She'd never really thought about the significance of this before. It turned out that her parents were very easygoing and, in her words, 'never encouraged me to meet new people, do exciting things or try to achieve anything more than being just average'.

The penny soon started to drop for Esther – she had grown into adulthood with the same approach. Like her parents, she couldn't help thinking that it was 'safer and more secure' to stay as you were rather than risk the dangers of trying new things. As a result, she'd always struggled to take a step into the unknown – she lacked the confidence to do this. She found it a huge relief to have found the answer and started to actively pursue new challenges in her life.

brilliant tip

Look further than just your experiences as an adult; think carefully about your childhood and the influences you came under.

It works the other way too:

▶ brilliant example

Ashley

Ashley couldn't work out why he never felt satisfied with his achievements. To his friends, 32- year-old Ashley was a successful web designer who had built up his own small company – he had his own company office with five people working for him. He was also a very talented sportsman.

He wasn't happy though. He knew this was something to do with his self-belief but couldn't quite put his finger on it. He thought back about his life and tried to work out if anything might have caused this. Like Miles and Esther though, he couldn't identify anything specific. Eventually he started to reflect on his upbringing.

He remembered that his father was 'incredibly ambitious' and that he had always expected Ashley to do well. He still remembered his father's favourite saying – 'Good isn't good enough Ashley ... excellent is where you need to be'.

Ashley was encouraged to play tennis from the age of five. He didn't mind this because he really enjoyed tennis. In fact, in his teens he played tennis for his county and won quite a few titles. However, even this success was never quite good enough for his father.

Eventually, Ashley started to lose his self-confidence and withdraw into himself. He couldn't reconcile why his father never seemed to be satisfied, even though Ashley thought he'd done well. Eventually he gave up tennis when he was 16.

As an adult, Ashley reflected back and thought about how his father's approach had affected him, he began to realise that in fact he'd achieved a huge amount in his life so far. This simple exercise in looking back helped him to believe in himself, feel satisfied with his achievements and be more self-confident.

So what?

Miles, Esther and Ashley all learnt lessons by reflecting on how the attitudes of their parents had affected them in later life. It wasn't until they were encouraged to think about this that they realised the impact their childhood had had on them. Sometimes, we just accept certain behaviour to be normal when actually it is anything but. This is only to be expected when we haven't had an opportunity to experience behaviour that's any different – more often than not, this happens when we are young and protected by our parents from other influences.

But as we grow out of childhood, we become more aware of our surroundings. What people think of you starts to matter. You can't help but compare yourself to your peers. It starts to mean something to you when the realisation hits that you aren't as good at something as someone else. At this point, your self-belief can start to wane and, if you let it get the better of you, before you know it you're on the slippery slope to losing your self-confidence. What's worse, if someone criticises you, you take it to heart; if you fail at something, you feel embarrassed.

Realistically, we can't bring back that natural free spirit and enthusiasm that we used to have when we were young but we can certainly try to emulate it. Confident people can do this – they don't let their concerns about what other people think affect them. This helps them to maintain the drive, enthusiasm and determination that we all used to have as children.

confident people don't let their concerns about what other people think affect them

Keeping the balance

The three Brilliant Examples above reflect what could be described as 'negative attitudes'. Of course, when reflecting on your childhood, you will have remembered positive experiences and fun times too. Don't forget these – a tremendous amount can be learnt from those fun experiences you had as a child.

brilliant tip

Ask yourself how much your lack of self-belief and self-confidence may originate from your experiences and relationships when you were young.

Adulthood

So, you've reflected on your childhood. You've probably turned over a few stones that haven't been touched for a long time. You might have discovered something just as Miles, Esther and Ashley did. Your discovery may well have been different to their experiences. Whatever it was, think positively about it and see it as a learning experience. Never let it be a weight around your neck.

On the other hand, it may be that you haven't discovered anything about your childhood that helps to explain your lack of self-confidence at this point in your life. Don't worry – all is not lost ...

Try thinking now about your life after you left home. What's happened since then?

Have you ever looked back and tried to identify actual events that happened or experiences you've had that may have had a knock-on effect on your confidence and self-belief? Well, this is definitely worth doing. Some people can remember a specific event that had a catastrophic impact on their confidence; others remember a series of smaller events that contributed; others can't really remember anything in particular but subconsciously know that past events have affected their confidence levels.

↗ brilliant exercise

Distant memories

Think back on your life. Think back as far as the time when you remember being more confident than you are now. If you think you've always lacked confidence, then reflect on the whole of your adult life.

Write down experiences you've had or events that have taken place that knocked your confidence levels and self-belief. If you can identify these, you've taken the first step to dealing with the negative impact they may have had. It never ceases to amaze me how important this exercise can be for some people. It's an exercise I encourage everyone who lacks self-confidence, self-belief or self-esteem to try.

Identify as much detail as you can about each memory:

● What happened?

● Why do you remember it?

● What can you learn from it?

Don't rush the exercise – you might not remember every experience straight away. Try mulling over it for a little while.

Some people come up with quite a comprehensive list of experiences; others only identify one major event. Try not to read on until you're happy you've had a good think about this.

Some of the following examples might help to jog your memory.

brilliant example

Martha

Martha attended a confidence-building training course.

From the minute she arrived she was incredibly warm and friendly. In fact, to me she seemed very confident and for a while I wondered why she'd come. I almost asked her if she was in the right room! I noticed that she had a slight speech impediment and wondered if this might have something to do with the reason.

Everyone had a chance to introduce themselves. When it was Martha's turn she became very emotional. We were all astonished to hear that she felt her confidence had been completely blown away by just one very clear experience she'd had.

She'd been to a job interview six months before. She'd explained to the panel at the beginning of the interview that she used a hearing aid because she was partially deaf. This also meant that sometimes she didn't realise she was speaking louder than others and perhaps not quite as clearly.

She thought the interview had gone well because at the end, two of the three people interviewing her gave her some very positive feedback and seemed happy. However, the third person on the panel (who happened to be the managing director) told Martha in a very direct and insensitive way that he thought she came across aggressively and therefore wouldn't fit in very well in their company. She was absolutely devastated – no one had ever described her as aggressive. She hated the thought of this because she prided herself in being a caring and sensitive person. All through her life she had worked in counselling type roles and now she was being told she was aggressive – in her mind this meant she was totally unsuited to what she wanted to do.

Martha couldn't stop this experience affecting her mental attitude and approach to life. The more she thought about it, the more she lost her confidence until eventually, luckily, one of her friends suggested she needed to get some help.

During the training course she attended with us, she began to realise that it wasn't *her* that had the problem with aggression – it was the managing director. He had totally misread her. In his mind, she had come across as aggressive because she had to speak quite loudly because of her partial deafness. It was only during the training course that she started to realise that it was *his* behaviour that was wrong, not hers.

For the past six months Martha had focused on that one event – one person telling her one thing about herself. She'd completely forgotten that the other two people on the panel had told her she'd done really well. She'd also completely forgotten all the other successes she'd had in her counselling career and the positive things people had said about her. Martha had let this one negative event completely take over her life and blow her confidence away. It took a whole day (the duration of the course) for us to convince her that in fact, it was the MD who had the problem, *not her*! He had completely misinterpreted her.

She walked away from the course as the person she used to be – looking forward to applying for interviews and to getting a new job.

---

brilliant tip

Try to get things in proportion. Don't let isolated events or experiences overpower your mindset. Confide in people who you know well and respect; explain to them the situation exactly as it happened and ask them how they interpret it. They may well see it differently to you. Then – very importantly – *believe* them.

You may have to think back quite a long way to pinpoint an experience that has affected your self-confidence. So keep an open mind here – don't make the assumption that only recent events are significant.

brilliant example

Josh

I met Josh in November 2009. He was really struggling with his confidence levels. You wouldn't know this necessarily because he came across well when you met him and talked to him. He just seemed a little shy.

He was a big man physically and must have been in his mid-forties. He told me that he knew exactly when it was that he'd started to lose his confidence. It all revolved around a sporting injury he'd suffered.

He told me he used to play squash for England. He told me that he had broken his foot and as a result he'd had to completely give up the sport. This had absolutely devastated him because his whole life revolved around squash. He had nothing to focus on anymore, nothing to feel proud about and, what's more, he'd lost touch with his friends, almost all of whom came from the squash circuit.

I couldn't reconcile the fact that his physical build just didn't match that of a squash player. It was only when I asked him when the injury had happened that it started to make sense – I nearly fell off my chair when he said '14 May 1988'.

For 21 years, Josh had been letting his injury affect his self-belief and confidence. Only now could he see what an impact it had had on his life and how he needed to move on.

Both Josh and Martha had specific experiences they could identify. With the help of friends, they were able to move on. Try to identify the significance of experiences like these quickly so that you can come to terms with them. Otherwise you'll get stuck like Josh did. Martha was different; she managed to deal with the issue within months because she addressed it.

In short, when casting your mind back, consider these rules (and stick to them):

- Identify the experience.
- Accept it/come to terms with it.
- Learn from it.
- *Forget it.*

It could be that, having reflected, you remember a series of small events that have taken place and affected your confidence; there might not necessarily be one big event that overcomes every-

don't dwell on the past for any longer than you need to

thing else. That's fine – the principle remains the same. Don't dwell on the past for any longer than you need to.

Experiences you can learn from

Once you've identified it, don't forget the experience until you're sure you've learnt from it. Josh and Martha's experiences required them to change their mindset – there was nothing specific they could learn from them other than that, in future, they needed to be strong enough mentally not to let such experiences affect them.

You might not be able to remember a specific event like they did. Perhaps you've had a number of experiences, all of which have led to a dip or in your confidence or self-belief. If so, it might be helpful to list them – is there a theme to them? Do they tend to relate to your social life or your work life? Do they revolve around the same kind of situation? For example, some people find that every experience they've listed relates to a situation when they are socialising and meeting new people. Others find that the experiences are specifically to do with work, perhaps attending meetings or giving presentations.

Regardless of what you come up with and uncover, the same rules apply. Having identified and come to terms with the experiences (and possibly a theme), now ask yourself what you can learn from them. What went wrong? What went right? In asking yourself these questions, you're looking for the answers to these two questions:

● Would it be worth trying to pre-empt and prepare better for the situation next time?

● What might I benefit from doing differently next time?

Finding the answers to these two questions will set you well on the way to building your self-confidence. We'll come back to this theme later when we deal with preparation.

Accepting your personal challenge

The fact that you're reading *Brilliant Confidence* suggests you've already decided you need to boost your confidence levels. It's great that you've taken the first major step on the road. Some people get stuck in a groove and don't manage to get this far.

There are two questions you should ask yourself at this point:

● Do you *really* want to change?

● Are you prepared to accept that you'll need to do some things differently from now on?

Be honest with yourself when you answer these questions. They could be the difference between success and failure.

You might be slightly unsure, particularly with regard to the second question – after all you don't yet know what the change involves. Don't worry about that for the moment – right now it's just important you realise that feeling and coming across as more confident will *definitely* mean doing some things differently. You'll need to accept that this might be difficult. You'll probably have to break some habits, possibly habits of a lifetime. No one ever finds this easy.

> you'll probably have to break some habits, possibly habits of a lifetime

But don't get the wrong idea here. Don't start getting depressed! These comments are designed to prepare you for the challenge ahead. 'Challenge' is a very appropriate word for this. You should see your endeavours to build your confidence as exactly that – a challenge.

Try to think of your journey to greater confidence as a personal project; your 'Confidence Project'. As with all projects it will only succeed if it is planned and prepared for thoroughly. The project needs to have a clear objective which is measurable – i.e. 'to achieve something by a certain date'. It helps to start thinking like this. For example – your strategic, long-term objective is to build your self-confidence. You've probably already worked that out. But have you thought about how that new self-confidence is going to show itself? Have you thought about what you're going to do with it once you have it? If you haven't, you're missing a trick.

After all, it would be daft to pass your driving test with flying colours and then get in your car with no idea of where you're going!

You'll need to break down your strategic objective into smaller chunks. Each of these chunks will have its own more tactical goals. *Brilliant Confidence* is written in a logical way. You'll be able to set your tactical goals as you progress through the book. Accepting your personal challenge becomes a lot easier if you take small steps at a time.

So, if you approach your Confidence Project on an incremental basis, the whole challenge will feel more manageable. Try approaching each chapter as shown in Figure 1.1.

This process will really help you to achieve your ultimate objective. Once you get the hang of it, you'll see how helpful the process is. *It makes you act*, rather than just read the book.

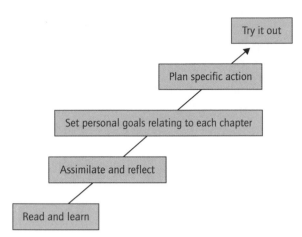

Figure 1.1 Approaching your Confidence Project: a road map

Starting your Confidence Project

To get started, think about the situations where your lack of confidence lets you down. You're trying to identify situations in which you feel most out of your comfort zone. These could be 'everyday' situations or they could be more significant specific events. They could have happened as a 'one-off' or they could be experiences that you have regularly. Cover both your personal life and your work life. Try to keep the two separate because you might decide to deal with them differently. The first step to dealing with a problem is to identify the issue.

brilliant exercise

Stumbling blocks

You'll need to write down and record each situation or event you find difficult so that it becomes a focus for you. As you move on through *Brilliant Confidence*, these stumbling blocks are going to form a major part of your Confidence Project.

Try to include as much detail as possible – break each situation or event down and try to cover the following:

- Describe the situation or event. (Example – networking events at work.)
- Describe why you find these difficult. (Example – because I don't know anyone and find it difficult to talk to people I haven't met before.)
- Describe what you think you do physically to show your lack of confidence. (Example – try to avoid people, let other people talk, feel uncomfortable with silences, look nervous, fidget, waffle.)
- Describe how you feel inside. (Example – pathetic, embarrassed, insecure, uptight, frustrated.)

brilliant tip

The first step to dealing with a problem is to identify it.

Now look to the future.

Think about how you would like to feel when you find yourself in the same situation again. Be positive and ambitious here – have some belief in yourself.

Write your thoughts down. Don't read on until you've finished.

Perhaps you've come up with something like this: 'When I go to my next networking meeting, I would like to feel confident, in control, relaxed, at ease and I would like to enjoy myself.'

> if you don't aspire to something, you won't have a focus; if you don't have a focus, you'll *never* achieve it

Great! You're now thinking positively. To succeed with the *Brilliant Confidence* ethic, you *must* start as you mean to go on. It's absolutely true that if you don't aspire to something, you won't have a focus; if you don't have a focus, you'll *never* achieve it.

Now you are all set up. You know the situations that are troubling you and you have a vision of how you would like to feel in the future. There's just one more thing that you'll need to come to terms with before we move on: your mind – is it working for you or against you?

CHAPTER 2

Being and feeling more positive

Having a positive mental attitude

'It is not the mountain we conquer but ourselves.'

Sir Edmund Hillary, mountaineer and explorer

Doubters beware!

Before you continue here, it's important that you open your mind to what you are going to read.

It might help if I let you into a secret. I used to be a person who didn't believe in positive thinking. I used to think that people who talked about thinking positively were just kidding themselves. I was convinced they were just playing mind games with themselves.

I remember thinking that surely they must be confused if they really believed that the simple act of just *thinking positively* would help them. How wrong I was. In fact, it wasn't until I started studying the subject and trying some of the concepts out for myself that I realised. I regret not keeping an open mind.

There's no doubt that not everyone accepts or believes in positive thinking. So, if you are a doubter, bear with me here – remember, I too was a sceptic once. Accepting that positive thinking works is the first step, only then can you start to consider how to achieve it and then how to use it effectively to build your confidence.

And don't forget – it's absolutely true that optimistic people are more likely to stay healthy and live longer than pessimists!

We know this because researchers at the University of Pittsburgh studied data from the Women's Health Initiative, an ongoing study of 100,000 women over 50 that started in 1994. At the beginning of the study, participants were asked to respond to whether they agreed with a statement like 'In uncertain times, I expect the worst'. Eight years later, researchers examined the women's death rates and found that those who were optimistic were 14 per cent more likely to be alive than the pessimists.

Where do you stand?

How do you describe yourself when someone asks you if you are a positive or negative thinker? If you're not sure, it's important to be clear on this before moving on.

Try asking yourself if you see your glass as half full or half empty. If it's half full, you're thinking the right way; you're likely to think more positively. If more often than not you see it as half empty, then you need to start trying to change your mindset straight away.

If you're still not sure where you stand here, try looking back over the last year – ask yourself what you remember. You'll probably have a mixture of good and bad memories. The key here is to establish which ones are taking precedence. Where does your focus tend to be? If you're thinking mainly of good experiences, well done – you're thinking positively. If you're thinking mainly of negatives, you need to start thinking about trying to shift your mindset.

We've already established during Chapter 1 that negative memories have value if you can learn from them. Once that's happened and you've squeezed out everything you can learn from them, you *must* forget them and move on. Confident people have the self-discipline to do this. They understand the dangers of constantly thinking back to negative experiences. They won't let these negative memories overpower the positives times. In essence, confident people think *positively* all the time.

> ## confident people think *positively* all the time

Achieving it

'I don't think of all the misery but of the beauty that still remains.'

Anne Frank, *The Diary of a Young Girl*

Positive thinking is a state of mind. It is a mental attitude that helps to steer your mind towards thoughts and actions that are conducive to self-belief and confidence. People who demonstrate a strong mental attitude and positive mindset anticipate and look forward to fulfilment and happiness. Their self-belief and positive attitude anticipates and expects success, not failure.

Have a think about people you know who you would describe as positive thinkers – I'll bet you would also describe them as having self-belief and self-confidence. That's because the two go together. The majority of confident people think positively.

So how do they manage to do this? Confident people do a number of things that help them to stay positive in their attitude. You'll see that these things are not complicated. In fact they are very simple and sometimes quite subtle. You should be able to try them out yourself straight away. But manage your expectations and be realistic. Don't get too carried away – attitude and thoughts take time to change. It's not going to happen overnight.

brilliant tip

People who lean towards negative thinking tend to forget the good things they do or that happen to them. You should remind yourself of these regularly, otherwise they'll get lost in a cloud of negativity.

So how can you start to help yourself to become more optimistic and to think more positively?

🔍 brilliant exercise

Homework

Each night before you go to bed, try writing down three positive things that happened or that you did during the day. This will help you to keep them in the forefront of your mind. Do this every night for the foreseeable future.

Some people find it helpful to buy a small notebook for this. This will make it easier to keep the list together and to reflect on the positives you record. It won't be long before you have a comprehensive list. Use this list to remind yourself regularly of the positives in your life. This is one small exercise that will help to keep you thinking positively.

Eliminate negative thoughts

Come to terms with where you stand here. If you tend to think negatively, don't let it happen. When a negative thought comes into your mind, be aware of it, then try to replace it with a constructive one. The negative thought probably won't go away easily, so persevere each time it enters your mind; make sure you replace it with a positive one every time it happens. Eventually your mind will learn how to think positively and ignore negative thoughts.

Try to do this even when your life isn't going as you would like it to or when you're worried about something. This will be the hardest time to think positively because negative thoughts will be most prominent. Train your mind to expect only positive results – believe that, at some point, your life will change for the better. You can speed this process up if you really want to.

brilliant tip

Write it down every time a negative thought comes into your mind. Sometimes you don't realise how much you're doing it until you actually see it in black and white.

Don't forget that positive and negative thinking are contagious. A negative attitude can show itself in your body language. This tends to happen on a subconscious level but can still have a significant impact on others. For example, socially, people don't tend to want to be around negative thinkers because they find them depressing; they find positive people more exciting and interesting. So, negative thinking can have an impact on your friendships and ultimately your social life too.

> positive and negative thinking are contagious

Your work life can also be dramatically affected; negative people aren't seen as people with potential and therefore are less likely to be promoted. Just think about it – how many successful business people do you know who think negatively? The answer must surely be none.

brilliant tip

Stop negative thinking; if you think you're going to fail, you'll feel like a failure; if you feel like a failure, you will fail.

Stop negative language

Of course, if you *think* more positively, the likelihood is that your message will be more positive when you speak it; that should come naturally. Watch out though, because you could have a habit of saying things that aren't helping you.

brilliant example

Costas

Costas was working for a merchant bank and had gone through their graduate training scheme. He was now in his third year as a full-time employee.

He'd recently had a performance appraisal and his manager had told him he thought he lacked self-confidence. His manager said he 'couldn't put his finger on it' but there was something about Costas that he felt portrayed a lack of confidence.

Costas agreed with him because he too felt his confidence could be boosted and they decided to book him on to a confidence-building training course. So, Costas arrived on the course and within 30 seconds he started saying something that portrayed him as person who lacked confidence. He was a serial 'sorry sayer'. He would apologise for everything. First he apologised for being late, even though he was in fact five minutes early – he just felt that he was letting the others down because they had arrived earlier than him. Then he apologised for sitting down because he wondered if someone else would prefer his seat. Then he said sorry for introducing himself because he wondered if anyone else might like to talk before he did. He would then apologise every time he wanted to ask a question. Almost everything he said was prefixed by the word 'sorry'.

The start of the course was about discovering why you lack confidence and why others perceive you as lacking confidence. When Costas was told, he was surprised to hear that that he said sorry a lot. He really didn't have any idea!

We told him each time he said sorry as the day went on. Most of the time, he wasn't even aware that he'd done it – it had become such a habit for him. He found this to be a massive learning experience. I'd been making notes and by the end of the day he'd said sorry 59 times! Not one of those times was necessary.

You might not think it but what you say does have an impact on how positive (or negative) you actually feel. Some people really struggle to come to terms with this. Confident people speak positive language. This helps them to stay positive in their mental attitude.

Saying sorry when an apology isn't appropriate sends negative signals to your mind. It also communicates a submissive message to the other person. It isn't a positive and confident action and therefore isn't conducive to developing self-belief and self-confidence. If taken to an extreme it can also lead to feelings of insecurity and inferiority.

brilliant tip

Don't say sorry unless it would be impolite not to or unless you've actually hurt or offended someone. Confident people are polite but only say sorry when an apology is warranted.

Here's a question for you: when someone asks you a question like 'How are you?' or 'How are things going?' what do you say in reply? Think carefully about this because you probably have a standard reply regardless of how you're actually feeling. People who don't make a conscious effort to think positively tend to reply to this question in a negative way. They'll say 'Not bad, thanks' or 'OK, thanks' in an unenthusiastic way. You're not going to sound and feel confident and positive when you reply like this (try saying it now to yourself and you'll see what I mean). If you have a negative mindset, a reply like this becomes your normal reply, *even* when you're having a *good* day! Why on earth would you want to give the impression things are only going 'OK' or things 'aren't too bad' when actually things are good? That's just silly.

So, how about being more positive the next time someone greets you and asks how things are going. Try saying 'Good, thanks' or if you really want to push the boat out 'Really good, thanks'. You'll be amazed at how much more positive you start to feel simply by speaking positive language. This really does work – you'll have to try it to see.

Of course, not only do *you* feel more positive – the person you're talking to sees you as a positive person and will subconsciously register this. The person is much more likely to want to help you, work with you, socialise with you, listen to you ... and the list goes on.

brilliant tip

Start practising your new reply when someone asks you how you are. Keep practising because breaking an old habit is never easy. Watch the person's face carefully – you'll see a more positive reaction from now on! This is bound to help you to stay positive yourself.

You might have read these points about negative language and thought they are not relevant to you. You wouldn't be the first person to do this. A word of warning here: *be careful* ... don't presume you don't think negatively because sometimes people just can't see or hear it in themselves. Costas was a perfect example.

Apologising unnecessarily is just one example of negative language. There are others too ...

brilliant example

Julie

Julie was conscious that she seemed to be bumbling through life. Although she enjoyed her job as a post lady, she was getting bored. Furthermore, her life had been turned upside down about six months earlier because, out of the blue, her husband told her he was leaving her after 12 years of marriage. This had really knocked her back.

Julie got more and more depressed and became very introverted although, in fact, she was quite a bubbly and extroverted person normally. When she explained her predicament and talked generally about her situation she couldn't see that her language was overwhelmingly negative. She had a habit of saying particular words and phrases that had a negative connotation. For example, one of her favourite phrases was 'if only'.

She had no idea that this was handicapping any possibility of her achieving a positive mindset. Her whole demeanour, even her body language, exuded this negativity.

The most frustrating thing for Julie was that she knew what she wanted to do with her life. Her plan was already in her mind. She wanted more independence – she wanted to be her own boss. She loved interior design and wanted to buy and sell property. She had some capital from the divorce and a property sale. With no children and no other responsibilities, she knew in her heart of hearts that, really, there should be nothing stopping her buying her first property.

The problem was that she was continually putting barriers up for herself because of her negative language. She just couldn't see what effect this was having on her mental attitude and mood – she needed other people to tell her.

Unless someone knows you very well (and even then it's doubtful), people aren't just going to volunteer information. Understandably, they'll worry about hurting your feelings or appearing rude. So, the best way to get someone to give you some feedback is to invite them.

brilliant exercise

Talk the talk

Try asking a good friend or relation to help you here. Ask them to tell you every time you say something negative. You might get a surprise! Give them some feedback on their language as well of course – they might learn something they didn't know too.

Once you know if you have a habit of saying something in particular, make a conscious effort to listen to yourself while you're speaking. This should help you to kick the habit.

Worriers

We all worry on occasions – it's only natural. However, some people are able to control their worries and not let them interfere with their lives to any great extent. It's true that some people are more 'easygoing' than others but even they worry sometimes. Unfortunately, if you're a 'natural worrier', you'll have to work harder on this than they might.

Controlling the effect that worrying has on your mental attitude is a vital component of maintaining a positive mindset. The simple way to do this is to have the self-discipline to keep your worries *in proportion*.

> have the self-discipline to keep your worries *in proportion*

Natural worriers always have to have something to worry about. If there's nothing major to worry about in their life at the time, they'll worry about something small.

▶ **brilliant** example

Christian

Christian told us this story during a confidence-building session.

He'd been staying with friends and was preparing for a long drive home. He got up early and packed his bag ready to go. He filled a flask with coffee, grabbed his bag and got into the car.

Half an hour later he was driving along and realised he'd forgotten his flask. It was too late to turn back because he had to catch a ferry which otherwise he would miss. Christian was a natural worrier – he just couldn't get the flask out of his mind. It wasn't just the fact that he'd forgotten it and wouldn't be able to drink the coffee in it. He couldn't help worrying about all the other implications of leaving the flask. He just couldn't get it out of his mind. He worried about not having it for his fishing trip next weekend; he worried about not having it for his son's rugby match on Wednesday; he worried that he wouldn't have it if he broke down … and in fact, that's exactly what happened – he did break down. Of course, at that point, he completely forgot about his flask. He had something else to worry about now – something probably worthy of a little bit of worry.

It was an interesting lesson for him – once he'd reflected on it he could see how out of proportion his worrying was.

☼ **brilliant** tip

Try to get your worries in perspective. Think about the worst thing that could possibly happen, then scale down and down again. Think about what's worrying you right at this very moment while you're reading this. Is it really that bad? Confident people get their worries in proportion.

The balance in life

It's difficult to think positively if you don't feel you have a balance in your life. Confident people have something about them that suggests they are in control of their lives. They have found an acceptable balance between their responsibility to others and their own wants and needs. This helps them to feel satisfied and to stay positive.

Importantly, they are also *realists* – they have come to terms with the fact that we all have responsibilities. For example, the majority of people have to work to earn a living. Most confident people accept this and get on with it.

You'll struggle to stay positive if you don't feel in control and satisfied with your life. A lot of people who lack self-confidence feel it's selfish to think of themselves. This is just not true; confident people realise that balancing your own wants, needs and aspirations with your responsibility to others is vital.

---

brilliant exercise

Life balance

Even if, on the face of it, you feel satisfied with the balance in your life, try this exercise. Be realistic though – for example, don't kid yourself that you aren't happy because you spend more time at work than you do on holiday!

It's important that you open your mind and think creatively, particularly when you're thinking about yourself and the things you would like to do or achieve. Ask yourself if the balance in your life is right. Try thinking about how much time you spend at work and then consider the other aspects of your life that are or should be important to you.

This is a personal and private exercise and only you will know what's important to you. It might help to think in terms of:

- your responsibility to others (work, family etc.)
- your responsibility to yourself (work, enjoyment, health, hobbies etc.).

It might be helpful to make a few notes on what you come up with. We'll refer back to this exercise later.

Staying healthy and keeping fit

If you're out of shape, there's more chance you'll feel insecure and unattractive. By keeping in reasonable shape, you'll improve your physical appearance and feel more energetic.

Of course, this doesn't happen on its own. You'll need to make the effort to achieve it. It's true that there is a direct link between your physical state and your mental state. The healthier you are, the easier it is to maintain a positive mental attitude.

Consider this on two levels:

- your general health
- your physical fitness.

> the healthier you are, the easier it is to maintain a positive mental attitude

General health

With the exception of illnesses over which you have no control, everyone should be able to stay healthy. If you're sensible with your diet and keep it balanced, if you ensure your body isn't physically stressed, if you get enough sleep and you get exercise, then you should be able to stay in good general health. If one of these key requirements is missing due to your lifestyle, you should think about making a change – you'll struggle to stay positive otherwise.

Physical fitness

It's also important to keep physically fit. Don't worry though, you don't have to be superfit – you just need to keep your body in trim. This is harder for some people than others due to physique and dietary considerations. But *everyone* can do it

– it just takes self-discipline. You need to find a realistic level of fitness that suits *you*.

This is worth trying if you haven't tried it already. Of course, 'physical fitness' means different things to different people. Don't worry about other people – don't try to match others unless you feel it would help. Manage your expectations here and do what *you* feel comfortable with. For one person this could mean walking 20 minutes a day; for another it could mean running for 20 minutes a day.

There are all sorts of fitness regimes you could consider – too many to list here. Do some research on the internet and pick one that suits you. You might also consider joining a gym, perhaps even joining a club. It doesn't have to be a running club – it could be any type of sport or perhaps a walking club. Start off slowly and work up; don't challenge yourself too much at the beginning.

Finding your focus

Understanding what drives you

To feel confident and in control of your life, you need to know what drives you; you need to know what makes you tick. Knowing what you actually *need* to keep you enthusiastic about life is an essential component of personal motivation. Knowing what you *need* is much more important than just knowing what you *want*. Needs are essential requirements, wants are desirables. There's a significant difference here in relation to feeling and being confident.

> knowing what you *need* is much more important than just knowing what you *want*

In simple terms, if you don't get what you want, you'll probably feel sorry for yourself and perhaps frustrated. That's not great but it isn't the end of the world – you should still be able to overcome this with self-discipline. However, if you don't get what you *need*, you'll come to a grinding halt.

↗ brilliant exercise

Personal motivators

Below is a list of 10 aspects of life that people feel are important to them. Look through them and think about them in terms of what you *need* in life, not so much in terms of what you *want*. Most people know themselves well enough to be able to differentiate between the two. Then rank each aspect of life in terms of its importance to you: mark the most important as 1, through to the least important, 10. If you want to discuss your answers with someone else, don't do this until you've completed the list, otherwise they might distract you from your personal thoughts.

_____ Enjoyment

_____ Interesting work

_____ Religion

_____ Salary

_____ Personal development and learning

_____ Recognition and appreciation

_____ Job security

_____ Family

_____ Ambition

_____ Friends and relationships

Each individual is different; understanding which of these are most important to you personally is essential. Knowing this will help you to get your true priorities in order. Once you know this, you'll have a clearer focus and you'll be able to shape your life to accommodate it. If you don't know what drives you and keeps you motivated, you can't aspire to it and you can't provide it. If you can't provide it, you'll end up in a downward spiral. It's impossible to maintain a positive mindset if you're not getting what you need in life to keep you enthusiastic and motivated.

Most people have a rough idea of where their orientation tends to be. Be careful though, don't make any assumptions – you might be surprised to find that, deep down, you need something different to what you originally thought. Therefore it could be that you're not getting it, simply because you didn't know you needed it. Your mental attitude will suffer if this happens.

It's just as bad to feed yourself constantly with something you don't actually need. That would be like putting unleaded petrol in a diesel engine. You'll cause some serious damage; ultimately your engine seizes up and you break down. It's also a huge waste of time and effort – time you could have spent filling up with the right fuel and driving where you want to go.

Setting positive objectives and goals

'Begin with the end in mind.'

Stephen Covey, author and management consultant

Now that you have a clearer feel for what motivates you, it's worth thinking about what you want to achieve out of life. To feel confident, you need to be focused; focus brings satisfaction and a sense that you're not wasting your time. You might find it helpful here to refer to the notes you made during the 'Life balance' exercise.

Do you ever think seriously about what you want to achieve during your lifetime? Do you ever reflect and ask yourself if you're *making the most* of your life? Or are you like the majority of people – going from day to day, busily doing the things that need to be done but never really thinking seriously about why you're doing them?

People who make the most of their lives have a sense of purpose about them. They know why they do things. How do they know this? In short, because they are *focused*. They know what they want to achieve and they've worked out how to achieve it.

> people who make the most of their lives have a sense of purpose about them

This is essential to maintaining a positive mindset. You could start by asking yourself what you were doing five years ago. What's happened since then? What have you *achieved* since then? These questions should get you thinking about whether or not you're making the most of your life.

However, other than learning from your mistakes, looking back isn't going to help you *now*. That time has gone. Positive thinkers focus on the future – and that's what you *must* start doing if you want to build your self-belief and self-confidence.

You'll be glad to hear that's it's not difficult to do this. It does however require self-discipline to get the process moving.

🔼 brilliant exercise

Cornerstone

This 'Cornerstone' exercise is going to form a major part of your Confidence Project. Be prepared to take some time over it. It's important not to rush it. If you commit to it fully, it will achieve exactly what its name suggests – it will act as the strong cornerstone upon which your Confidence Project is built. The exercise involves a number of steps. Stop after each step to reflect – you might decide to change something on reflection.

Step 1 – Strategic thinking

Try projecting your thoughts into the future. You're looking between two and five years ahead. In other words, you're looking strategically at your life over a period of time. I find that younger people, say in their twenties or early thirties, sometimes prefer to look two or three years ahead – five years can seem like a long time at this age. This isn't always the case though, so choose a period of time that suits you. Remember, you're thinking strategically so it shouldn't be any less than two years.

It's important to differentiate between your work life and your personal life. We've already touched on the importance of achieving a balance to your life if you want to feel more confident and positive. Differentiating between work and personal life will help with this. Once again, referring to the notes you made during the 'Life balance' exercise will help with this.

Now start to open your mind and think about what you would like to achieve over this strategic period of time. Your ultimate aim here is to set some strategic objectives.

You'll need to make a few notes to get you started. Some people find it useful to create a 'mind map'. This is a simple creative thinking process which involves jotting down everything you can think of that has relevance to the strategic period you are looking ahead at in your life; consider your needs, your wants, your aspirations, your responsibilities, your family, your career – and anything else you think is important. Don't forget to reflect on the personal motivators list you filled in – remember, you worked out that you need certain drivers to keep you motivated, and they must be factored in.

Mind maps only work if you challenge yourself to be bold and imaginative. Don't be scared to write down your aspirations. This will help you to think creatively.

As an example, look at the mind map shown in Figure 2.1, developed by Orla, a participant on a confidence-building course. It gives you a feel for the concept. Your mind map should be personal to you.

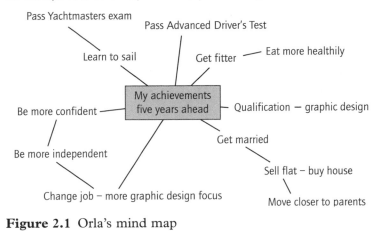

Figure 2.1 Orla's mind map

Step 2 – Strategic objectives

The strategic objectives you create here will form the platform upon which the next stage of your life is built. They are one of the key elements of your Confidence Project.

Having created your mind map, the next step is to use it to form strategic objectives. This converts the mind map into something meaningful. Think carefully about this – don't rush it.

It's important that you are realistic during this exercise. For each objective you set, you're striving for the balance between challenge and achievability. Yes, you should challenge yourself but don't be so ambitious that deep down you know you won't be able to achieve your objectives. If just one objective loses credibility, your enthusiasm to achieve the others will wane.

Each time you come up with an objective, ask yourself if you'll be able to assess whether or not you've achieved it. You won't be able to do this if it's not specific or if it's not measurable in some way. Don't forget the time aspect either. Yes, these are strategic objectives but that doesn't necessarily mean that every one of them is to be achieved over the five-year period. It may make sense to aim to achieve some of them over the shorter term. For this exercise, the shorter term shouldn't be less than two years though.

Here are *just some* of the strategic objectives Orla developed from her mind map. They give you a feel for the transition you need to make between the mind map and objective setting.

Career/Work life	Personal life
To study for and achieve a recognised graphic design qualification by March 2012.	To study for and pass Yachtmasters exam by December 2012.
To get a job in the graphic design sector by December 2012.	To sell flat and buy two-bedroom house near parents by end of 2012.
To set up my own graphic design consultancy by December 2015.	To run a half marathon by December 2011.
	To get married by August 2012.

You can see that Orla's strategic objectives are specific and measurable. She will know whether or not she's achieved each one because she can assess them. She hasn't finished yet though. She needs to start thinking shorter term or more 'tactically' now – she needs to focus on each objective in its own right and consider what needs to happen to get it moving.

Step 3 – Tactical thinking

This helps you to determine what you need to do in the shorter term to gets things moving. Tactical thinking bridges the gap between the present and the future. Let's take one of Orla's objectives as an example of how tactical thinking is employed.

One of her strategic objectives in her personal life is 'To run a half marathon by December 2011'. She's given herself two years to achieve this because at the present time she sees herself as generally unfit and doesn't do any running at all.

She's now thinking more tactically – so she's looking at the next six months. Each strategic objective has to be supported by tactical goals. Therefore, to support her fitness objective, she decides to set herself the following goals to be achieved over the next six months:

● To be able to jog 2 miles and to swim 10 lengths by the end of month 1.

● To be able to jog 3 miles and to swim 15 lengths by the end of month 2.

● To be able to jog 4 miles and to swim 20 lengths by the end of month 3.

● To be able to jog 5 miles and to swim 25 lengths by the end of month 4.

● To be able to jog 6 miles and to swim 30 lengths by the end of month 5.

● To be able to jog 7 miles and to swim 35 lengths by the end of month 6.

Step 4 – Personal action plan

Now that your tactical goals are clear, you need to put together a plan of action. This details what you have to do on a weekly basis in order to achieve these tactical goals.

Orla took it step by step. She concentrated on one month at a time – initially, she focused on the first week of month 1. She decided that to achieve the one-month goal, she would need to jog one mile twice and swim five lengths twice during the first week. She lived about a mile away from the swimming pool so she would jog there and back when she went.

Remember the sequence charted in Figure 2.2; it will stand you in good stead and provide you with a solid platform from which to work. Don't forget that finding your focus should be a continuous process. You're regularly reviewing it and setting new objectives and goals when others have been achieved.

Figure 2.2 The personal planning sequence

PART 2

First steps to confidence

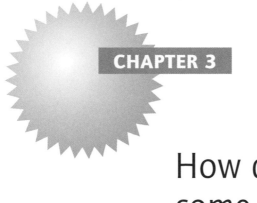

CHAPTER 3

How do you come across?

'It took me a long time not to judge myself through someone else's eyes.'

Sally Field, American actress

Have you ever thought about how people perceive you? I mean *seriously* thought about it? It's true that we all wonder what people think of us every now and then. But it's also true that we tend to wonder this through curiosity rather than for any constructive reason.

Getting to the bottom of how people perceive you is one of the essential elements of understanding how you come across to them. Once you know this, you can start to think about adapting your behaviour so that their perception of you is what *you* want it to be. To feel confident, you need to know how you look and sound; you need to know how you come across. You need to know how to control peoples' perceptions of you.

to feel confident, you need to know how you look and sound

Does it really matter what others think of you?

'Who cares what people think of me!' These might sound like the words of a confident person and to an extent the person is right to think like that. It's true that confident people don't worry as much as others might about what people think of them and how they come across. It's fine to think like this and be independent minded but it's dangerous to discount other people's perceptions of you completely.

To feel truly confident, it's important to understand the concept of perception and to take account of it when communicating. You need to be aware of people's perceptions of you but not let this cloud your judgement. If you let the concept of perception get the better of you, you could start to become paranoid.

People who disregard others' perceptions of them are missing a trick. It really does matter what people think and how they perceive you – but it shouldn't be the be all and end all. The reality of life is that most people can't help but be affected by other people's impressions of them and therefore how people react to them. This in fact is a positive thing if considered constructively. The important point to remember is that if you can control others' perceptions of you, you can control how they react to you.

Bear in mind that it can work the other way too. Most people who lack self-confidence make the presumption that people *perceive* them to lack confidence because of the way they look and act. This is not necessarily the case. Other people may in fact see you as a confident person! So – keep an open mind.

---

brilliant example

Claudette

Claudette walked into the room at the beginning of a confidence-building course. She sat down and looked comfortable straight away, even though she hadn't met any of the other people there before.

Each person introduced themselves and explained why they had come. Claudette explained very confidently that she had no self-confidence at all. She said she felt embarrassed whenever she had to talk to a group of people. She actually said 'This is a great example ... You can see it for yourself by the way I look now ... I'm just a bag of nerves.'

We then discussed how the group perceived each person in terms of self-confidence when they introduced themselves. Claudette was staggered to hear that, without exception, all the people in the room perceived her to be a confident person. She genuinely could not believe it. She thought people were trying to be kind because, really, they thought she was so awful. She'd built up such a strong false impression of how she looked and sounded that it took quite a while for us to convince her that we weren't trying to be nice – we were telling the truth.

Claudette was just one of many people I meet who've formed the wrong perception of themselves.

Try thinking of the perception process as shown in Figure 3.1. If you can control people's perception of you, you can make it work in your favour. In other words, if you can ensure that their perception is positive, they'll see you as a confident person; if you interpret their reaction to you as positive, interested, motivated, animated ... your confidence levels will rise – and of course it works the other way round too.

> if you can control people's perception of you, you can make it work in your favour

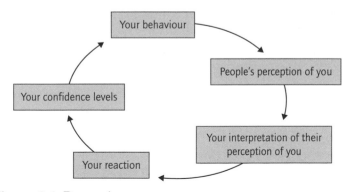

Figure 3.1 Perception process

Imagine if you're telling someone a story and in the middle they start yawning. This is bound to have an impact on you – after all, to most people, yawning indicates boredom or disinterest. If someone's expression suggests something negative about you, then this is bound to have an effect on your thoughts and behaviour – so for this reason it does matter what people think of you.

Confident people know how to process this negative information and how to react to it. They don't let this affect their *feelings*. If you can control your reaction so that it doesn't affect your emotions, then you can channel your efforts more effectively into dealing with the situation and being perceived as confident and in control.

So, if someone starts yawning when you're talking to them, it means something! You need to make a decision – if what you're telling them is important, you need to adapt your behaviour; you need to do something different because they're probably not listening properly. Some people find it helpful to say to themselves, 'I won't accept yawning when I'm talking to you'. This may sound a bit mad but it actually does work. It spurs you on to deal with the negative behaviour with confidence. Be careful though – make sure you don't say it out loud or it might backfire on you!

brilliant tip

Don't panic when someone appears to react negatively towards you. The situation can always be retrieved. Try to reflect, control your emotions, think positively and act with self-confidence.

Thick skinned?

Most people accept that other people's perceptions of them *do* matter.

Not all people though. Some people think that what others think of them is of no consequence at all. After all, 'confident people do their own thing'. They're right to some extent – however, they're not being very *clever*. Some might even say they're being over-confident – and that's dangerous territory to be in.

These people tend to be people we would describe as 'thick skinned'. They're just not bothered about what people think of them. Sometimes they even pride themselves in having this trait, this supposed 'strength of character'. It's true that they're lucky they don't get affected emotionally by what other people think of them – but, be under no illusion, that's where the benefit of being thick skinned stops.

---

brilliant example

David

David seemed like a very confident person. He spoke clearly and had no problem sharing his thoughts. We were talking during a coaching session about the concept of perception and how it related to self-confidence.

Pretty well before we'd even started, David blurted out that he just couldn't see the link between the two. As far as he was concerned 'It didn't matter a damn what other people think of you ... Surely confident people shouldn't be affected by other people's perceptions of them.'

David was a thick skinned person. He couldn't see that, although other peoples' perceptions don't affect the way *he* behaves, they do affect the way *others* behave towards him. Slowly, as we talked, he started to think about the possible implications of his disregard for other people's perceptions of him.

He'd worked as a security officer at an airport. He'd been performing the same role for six years and was keen to move into the operations team at the airport. He'd been telling his boss this for nearly six years. He knew there were opportunities to change role because he'd seen positions advertised on the internal email system. Eventually he started getting very frustrated because each time he asked his boss if he would put him ▶

forward, his boss told him he didn't think he would be 'suitable'. David couldn't work out what he meant.

After a while he decided to take things into his own hands and he applied for one of the new roles. He thought he'd done well at the interview and was shocked to hear subsequently that he'd been unsuccessful. The feedback from the interview was that his 'strong personality' didn't suit the new role; furthermore, they felt he hadn't listened to the questions properly before answering.

During our discussion, the penny started to drop for David. Only now did he realise that others perceived him to be 'cocky', 'inconsiderate', 'insensitive', 'selfish' and 'arrogant'. He was genuinely shocked to hear this. In fact, it started to dawn on him that his failure to take account of others' perceptions was impacting on the path of his life. He'd failed the interview as a result of it.

brilliant tip

Have the confidence to 'do your own thing' but *don't* disregard other people's perceptions of you. Factor this into your thought processes and actions. Take account of people's perceptions but don't let this turn into paranoia.

Seeing how others perceive you – any surprises?

What determines how people perceive you? Knowing the answer to this question is the first step towards making sure that someone's perception of you is the perception *you* want them to have.

We take in so many different messages while we're forming a perception of someone. Some messages are obvious to the eye or ear – for example, if someone quite obviously stutters as they speak and has a weak voice, you tend to form the perception that they are nervous or uncomfortable.

Obvious physical messages like nervousness in your voice are relatively easy to address, mainly because you are already aware of them – after all, if you know you're doing something wrong, it's just a case of working out how to do it right, and then putting it into practice. (We'll cover ways of stopping yourself sounding nervous later.)

It's the other more subtle messages that can be difficult to identify and, therefore, to address: the way you stand, your eye contact, the tone of your voice, your natural expression ... and the list goes on. We all have subtle behaviours that we have no idea we are portraying. These behaviours communicate under-lying messages that we have no idea we are sending. Some of these work in your favour – you might describe them as positive behaviours – for example if you have a posture which is naturally upright and open, you portray confidence. So this helps you to achieve what you want from the perception people have of you.

> we all have subtle behaviours that we have no idea we are portraying

Other behaviours aren't helping you at all though. It's these negative behaviours that need to be identified and addressed. People who are perceived by others as confident are good at this. They have an awareness about their behaviour. They know they are vulnerable to certain negative behaviours and they keep on top of them.

So, by now, you're probably wondering how you find out if you personally have any negative behaviours and habits that affect people's perception of you – well, if you're not, you should be!

Identifying negative perceptions

There's one obvious way to establish if you're doing anything negative and that's to ask people. We'll come back to this later. I'd like you to try something else first.

Have you ever tried to compare your own perception of yourself with the perception others have of you? This can be quite a revelatory exercise because people are often surprised to find that the two don't always match up. So, before you find out how other people perceive you (and before you start to cloud your own judgement with their perceptions), try this exercise.

⊅ brilliant exercise

Self-perception

Try coming up with your own perceptions of yourself. To do this, you'll need to write down every adjective that comes to mind when you describe yourself. You need to be comprehensive when you do this – be honest. This should be a private exercise, not to be shared with anyone else; that way you won't have to worry about the embarrassment of what others might think – being straight with yourself shouldn't be a problem.

It's important to consider all aspects of your life. This is because words that you use to describe yourself at work don't necessarily come to mind when you're describing yourself at home or when you're socialising.

You need to cover what you consider to be both *good* and *bad* about yourself. So, make two lists – one for the negative descriptive words and the other for the positive words. Take your time over this. Make sure you cover everything. Don't make the mistake some people make – they forget to write down the good points! No one will see what you write so there's no chance anyone will think you're boasting.

These two lists you've created are going to form a focus for you as you read on. We'll use them as a means of building on your strengths and dealing with your weaknesses. So don't lose them! You'll need them later.

One thing to say first though – your aim will be to eliminate the bad words – the negatives. No longer can you have these negative perceptions of yourself. Confident people only allow positive perceptions. This doesn't of course mean that confident people are perfect – nobody is perfect. It's just that confident people have the strength of mind to overcome any negative perceptions and deal with them before they have an impact.

> no longer can you have these negative perceptions of yourself

Don't forget, too, that some people form completely the wrong perception of what others around them think of them. In time, this can cause major problems if left to get out of control.

brilliant example

Sachin

Sachin was of Indian origin. His family educated him in the Middle East. He'd made the most of the opportunity and had left university with a first class degree in Economics. Having graduated, he returned to India and was employed by a well-known international bank.

Life was going well for Sachin. He had got married and had two children. By now he'd been working for the bank for six years and had responsibility for a team of 40 people. The bank saw him as a rising star. They offered him a role in the UK to build a new team with the same role as his Indian team. He decided to take it because it was another step on his career path. Also, the salary was better and he felt he could offer his family a better standard of living in the UK.

So the family emigrated and moved into a rented flat just outside London while they looked for a house to buy. Sachin began his new job but very quickly started to feel uncomfortable. His colleagues were very different to those in India. Whereas in India he had been the boss, now he worked on a par with people. He wasn't used to that.

▶

Sachin described his discomfort as a feeling of 'inferiority'. He couldn't think of anything specific that was causing this feeling, even when pushed. More and more he formed the impression that he was 'inferior' to others around him, even though he was better qualified and more experienced than most of them. He didn't feel there was anything racist about it, in fact the people he worked with were very nice. Eventually, he became demotivated and depressed. His work started to suffer and he struggled to recruit and build his team. The bank then demoted him.

We established during our discussion that Sachin had created this problem himself. With no substance at all to form a rational judgement, his perception of others had got the better of him. He'd found himself in a different culture to the one he was used to; people would approach him more directly and on occasions challenge him. This wasn't to check if he was good enough; it was just the way the UK operation worked. He wasn't used to this and as a result his perceptions of his colleagues were wrong in relation to the way they interacted with him. This caused his feeling of inferiority which eventually turned into an inferiority complex. It was totally unfounded because not only was he better qualified and more experienced than every one of his close colleagues, he was also studying for a Masters degree in his spare time.

Sachin lost all his confidence. This was incredibly frustrating and confusing because he knew that once, not so long ago, he had been a confident person. It went from bad to worse because his feelings of inferiority started to show themselves outwardly and eventually his colleagues (through no want or motivation of their own) started to view him and treat him as inferior.

He ended up moving jobs and accepted that he would have to take a cut in salary. He needed a change. It did him the world of good because it helped him to make a fresh start. With the help of personal counselling, he realised that his perception had got the better of him. It was totally wrong. He just needed someone to *tell* him. The difficulty had been that his feelings of inferiority had started to snowball once his mind turned negative. He saw everything negatively, even though, now that he looked back, he realised that a lot of the things that happened were in fact positive on his part in terms of his dealings with colleagues. He just couldn't see it at the time.

brilliant tip

Perception works in many ways. What you perceive of others is just as important as what they perceive in you. Don't make any assumptions – question your judgement regularly. If in doubt, think positively.

Inferiority

Sachin's perception of inferiority was specific to him. However, it does reflect a more wide-ranging problem. I find one of the main reasons people lack self-confidence is that they see around them a completely different world to the real one. They see the world as a place where everyone else is superior to them. They make the assumption that other people have more authority than them and that other's rights prevail above theirs.

It may well be the case that some people are more 'senior' to you in terms of position or rank. However, this does not mean that they are 'superior' to you in the sense that their rights and needs are more important.

Confident people treat everyone the same, regardless of rank or seniority. Of course, they show the appropriate degree of respect to seniors but they don't change their behaviour. People who feel inferior tend to lose sight of this. They forget that senior people

confident people treat everyone the same, regardless of rank or seniority

have no 'rights' over you, even though, particularly in a work environment, they may have a degree of 'power' over you in terms of your role and responsibilities.

brilliant tip

Always remember that you are on a par with everyone else. Be professional and polite and try to treat everyone the same. Approach a senior person with the confidence you would approach a peer.

I wouldn't be surprised if you're thinking that's easier said than done. After all, it's natural to feel a little daunted by the prospect of treating people who are senior to you as equals. It's actually not that difficult – but it does require mental preparation. The following exercise should help.

brilliant exercise

Equal terms

Think forward to the next time you might find yourself working or socialising with a group of people, some of whom are senior to you in some respect. Prepare yourself to treat them differently to the way you might normally. Whereas you used to treat them according to your perception of their authority in relation to you, now you will treat each of them as an equal. You will do this for everyone, even the people who are more 'senior' to you in terms of position. Don't worry, this won't be a problem as long as you're polite and respectful at all times.

You'll be amazed at how this simple concept can transform your sense of inferiority into a feeling of equality. You'll also be pleasantly surprised at the more positive way people respond to you, even the more senior people.

Sachin made a number of misjudgements on what others thought of him. His issue was inferiority. In another situation I've experienced, the issue was ugliness. I was coaching a person who thought she was ugly. Over the years, more and more, she managed to convince herself that she was ugly. Because she was so set in her mind regarding her self-perception, she then made the assumption that people's behaviour towards her always suggested that they thought she was ugly (when in fact they weren't thinking anything of the kind).

The ridiculous thing was that, to me, she seemed very attractive! I had to be careful how I told her this though!

Just ask!

Most people do wonder what people think of them every now and then. We've established that there's nothing wrong with wondering this. Actually, being aware of other people's perceptions of you is a vital component of feeling confident – it certainly doesn't mean you're vain or paranoid.

Have you ever taken it a step further and actually *asked* someone what they think of you? Not in terms of your morals or values, but in terms of how they perceive you specifically with regard to your confidence levels. You must try this – it's an essential crossroads on the journey to increased confidence.

brilliant exercise

Straight talking

Consider what you can learn from others' perceptions of you. Overcome your inhibitions and ask a person you know well to give you some honest feedback. Prepare how you're going to ask before you approach them – ▶

because of most people's nature, they'll want to be nice to you; they'll probably be reluctant to hurt your feelings.

So, make sure they know you're serious about getting some constructive feedback. Tell them why you want the feedback. Tell them they aren't going to hurt your feelings if they have negative things to say – equally, tell them they aren't going to embarrass you if they have good things to say.

Ask them confidently – don't start giggling or looking embarrassed. Ask them if they think you seem like a confident person; and if not, why not. If yes, why yes? You're looking for advice on your behaviour, your body language and your verbal language. You may well be surprised at what you hear – many people are. Hold yourself back if you disagree with them – don't forget, they are being honest with you. They can't help what they see in you.

You might consider asking them if they would like some feedback too – on your perception of them. If you're honest with them, they'll be honest with you. Be careful though if you do offer, because while some cultures are very open and accepting in their approach to receiving personal feedback, others are incredibly sensitive. You could cause offence in some cultures unless you approach it carefully.

There's another way of finding out people's perceptions of you too:

↗ brilliant exercise

The Think Confidence Reality Check

On our (website www.thinkconfidence.com) you can find out how others perceive you by asking them to complete our Think Confidence Reality Check. They'll give you feedback by completing an online questionnaire anonymously – their names won't appear, so you won't know who said what.

It's a great way of finding out how others perceive you in terms of how you come across. You'll need to nominate people who you think you know well enough to give you some balanced feedback. The Reality Check is comprehensive. It covers everything from people's first impression of you to whether or not people think they can depend on you.

Try to choose as wide a range of people as possible: good friends, members of your family, work colleagues, neighbours, etc. The more people the better – that way you'll get a good overall impression of how people see you. Make sure people know they're completing the questionnaire anonymously – they're more likely to record what they really think. They'll also see this when they read the instructions for completing the Reality Check on the website.

The Reality Check will only work if people are completely open and honest in their answers. Replies are collated confidentially online through the Think Confidence website and sent to you by email. You won't know who gave which replies about you, but you will gain a great insight into how others perceive you.

If you'd like to read more about the Think Confidence Reality Check, go to www.thinkconfidence.com/questionnaires.html

Filming

Being filmed is a great way of learning about how people see you. I always offer people who attend confidence-building courses the opportunity to be filmed. Very few people feel comfortable being filmed but, without exception, everyone finds it a revelatory exercise.

Receiving feedback verbally from people is very useful but there's nothing quite like seeing yourself in the flesh. It's interesting because pretty well everyone I film finds the exercise itself to be a confidence boost! Yes, I really mean this. People surprise themselves by coming across better than they thought they would. This is because most people have already *presumed* they'll look and sound awful. But it just doesn't work out like that. For example, it's often the case that people who thought they surely must have sounded very nervous realise that in fact they didn't sound nervous at all! It's also common for people who thought they waffled to see that in fact, they spoke clearly and didn't waffle at all!

> most people sound and look better than they thought they would

Don't get me wrong here. I'm not saying that everyone I film is brilliant at it – of course not. But what I'm saying is that most people sound and look better than they thought they would. They genuinely surprise themselves and this boosts their confidence immediately.

Of course, you don't have to pay for a training course in order to be filmed. Some people film themselves privately. Make sure you have a topic if you're going to do this. Prepare properly first. Or maybe you could ask someone else to film you (and give you some feedback at the same time). Perhaps you could combine this with a meeting you're going to or a presentation you're giving at work. Film yourself as you practise your presentation – it's a great way to rehearse too.

Being aware

Stay aware all the time. Don't ever switch off to how others might be perceiving you. You can learn a tremendous amount by just watching how people behave towards you and by listening to what they say and the way they say it.

Watch people's expressions and their body language. Listen to what they say to you and the questions they ask. It could be a very simple question that people ask you regularly which you hadn't even thought significant that gives away their perception of you. For example, if people ask you if you're 'OK' a lot, it probably means you don't look OK to them! You must be doing something for them to form that perception.

Personal effectiveness and discipline

Peoples' perception of how you come across to them isn't just based on how you look and sound. It's also based on how you behave and how you organise yourself. You'll feel more confident, and there's more chance people will perceive you as confident and in control, if they see you as an organised, tidy and efficient person.

Personal organisation

How many confident people do you know who are disorganised? If you can think of any at all, they tend to be the exception to the rule. Confident people are usually organised, both practically and mentally. There's a lot of truth in the saying 'disorganised desk, disorganised mind'.

> confident people are usually organised, both practically and mentally

If you tend to be disorganised in the way you run your life, you'll struggle to think clearly and logically. If you can't think clearly and logically, you'll let both yourself and others around you down. The result of course is that nothing people perceive in you is positive. At best they'll see you as messy and scatty; at worst they'll see you as lazy, unreliable, unprofessional, selfish ... and the list goes on.

The difficulty is that people won't necessarily tell you they see you like this, they'll just perceive it. More often than not, if they perceive it, you'll detect it in their behaviour towards you. As we've seen already, this could have a significant impact on your work and personal life.

So, when you started thinking about building your self-confidence, you might not have seen the link between personal organisation and confidence. Don't worry, you wouldn't have been the first person not to. The key now is to address the issue if you need to.

Managing your time

Being efficient and organised with the use of your time is essential. If you feel that your life is under control and that you're making the most of it, your sense of well-being will be stronger. This is bound to help with your personal self-belief in relation to what you would like to achieve.

Try asking yourself how you tend to approach life. Are you what is often referred to in 'time management language' as a Type A personality or a Type B personality?

- *Type A* – Describes people who like to get things done and push themselves quite hard. They'll cram a lot into their day. However, they sometimes take on too much and fail to set aside enough time for relaxation or reflection on where they are going.

- *Type B* – Describes people who work at a slower pace and are able to bring a healthy balance to their lives. They aren't so conscious of time deadlines. People who demonstrate extreme Type B behaviour often let others down because of their laid-back nature.

Having established where you see yourself on the Time Line (see Figure 3.2), consider whether or not you would benefit by changing your approach slightly. You might find that you fall between Type A and Type B behaviour. That's not unusual.

Figure 3.2 The Time Line

In fact, it's quite a nice place to be because you're not leaning towards either extreme.

Type A people tend to be late because they've got so many other things to do. Type B people may be late because they're just more relaxed about the concept of time. There are the obvious reasons for not being late, the main one being that you've let other people down and wasted their time. Some people naturally feel bad when they let people down, others don't. Ask yourself where you stand here.

So, what's this got to do with confidence? If you want to feel confident at all times, you'll need to have this considerate mentality built into your mindset.

Letting people down is a good enough reason on its own for not being late but there are other more personal reasons that can also have a direct impact on your confidence:

● If you're late, you're already on the back foot. The other person already sees something negative in you because you've let them down. You can't afford to project any negativity at all if you want to come across and therefore feel confident. If you're late, you now have a slope to climb created through your own making, rather than a level playing field.

● If you're late, you'll cause a distraction for yourself (and others). You'll be thinking about what people think of you rather than how you're coming across. You know you're late and this will be (or certainly *should* be) on your mind. You can't afford any distractions if you're trying to come across confidently. You need 100 per cent attention on the task at hand – i.e. to look and sound confident.

Wherever you find yourself on the Time Line, make the decision right now that you will endeavour never to be late again.

Of course, if you're delayed by events outside your control, then that's understandable. Don't forget to explain this though when you get there!

> ☼ **brilliant** tip
>
> Don't be late, don't even be on time – be slightly early. Then you've got time to prepare yourself to come across confidently. You'll be on the front foot (and already one step ahead of people who haven't yet arrived).

Any adjustments required?

Already in *Brilliant Confidence*, you've worked through a number of exercises. They'll all help to boost your confidence levels. You've probably also identified a number of things you would benefit from doing differently. In other words, you need to make some changes. This means making some adjustments to the way you behave. There are some simple things you can do to make this process as smooth as possible.

To feel confident and in control from this point on in your life you'll need *self-discipline*.

Don't let the 'gremlin' get you!

The gremlin is behind that tempting feeling you get every time you either feel lazy, you procrastinate or you half-do something. Think back here to the 'Stumbling blocks' exercise you completed in Chapter 1. You listed the situations you find difficult to deal with. Your gremlin will be having a field day when this happens. Your gremlin has won when it stops you doing something you know you should do.

The gremlin is the cause of many things relating to your lack of self-belief, self-esteem and self-confidence. For example:

● Your gremlin is to blame for trying to pull you back during those situations when you know you *should* actually be putting your view across confidently.

● Your gremlin will be trying to get in your way when a job comes up at work that you know you *should* do but don't feel comfortable doing.

● Your gremlin will be trying to hold you back when an opportunity arises that you haven't quite got the confidence to seize.

This gremlin can massively affect the way you come across to people. If you let it get the better of you, you'll be seen as a person who is at best unhelpful and at worst lazy and not worth having in the team. The knock-on affect of this on your self-confidence could be catastrophic.

Remember, your gremlin *is not your friend* and nice to have by your side to help you stay out of the limelight, or to make you feel better if you feel lazy. The gremlin is your enemy.

You will know the next time your gremlin tries to get you. Be aware it's happening and overcome it. It could be today, tomorrow or the next day. It could be at work or at home. Wherever and whenever it happens, *don't let the gremlin get you.* Dealing with the damaging influence of your gremlin is one of the keys to overcoming the personal stumbling blocks you identified.

> you will know the next time your gremlin tries to get you

Your gremlin never goes away completely but confident people know how to deal with it. They speak up when they've got something useful to say. They seize opportunities when they arise. They act when they know it's appropriate to do so. Self-discipline is the key to success here.

brilliant tip

Your gremlin is terrified of self-discipline, moral courage and organisation. Don't let it get you!

CHAPTER 4

How do you communicate?

We've established the importance of considering how you come across to others and the implications that differing perceptions can have. But when you drill down, what is it that people *actually* do that makes them *look* and *feel* confident? There's one word that sums this up in a nutshell – *communication*. This is the nucleus around which your ability to look, feel and be more confident revolves.

So far, we've looked at how your mindset can affect your behaviour and, to some extent, what you say – you'll remember Julie who was a negative thinker and said 'if only' a lot, and Costas who couldn't stop saying 'sorry'. What we haven't yet looked at is *how* you communicate.

You communicate in your own particular way – we all do. Over the years you've developed your own natural communication style. To feel confident and in control, you need to be aware of this style. It's essential that you know what's good and what's bad about it; in other words, you need to know your strengths and weaknesses in relation to how you communicate.

Some people like to be the centre of attention and to talk; others prefer to watch from the sidelines and to listen. Decisions such as these are determined both consciously and subconsciously through your natural communication style. This style is

you need to know your strengths and weaknesses in relation to how you communicate

your own personal way of communicating, the way you come across when you don't consciously think about it. It will suit certain situations but not others. That's why it's so important to get to the bottom of it. Otherwise, there's a good chance that, just by being your normal self and communicating in your natural way, without even realising it, you'll:

- make someone feel uncomfortable
- distract them from your message
- appear rude to them
- appear boring and disinterested
- look like a person who lacks confidence.

the secret is to think about adapting your style

Once you know your natural style, you can make sure these negative perceptions don't arise. The secret is to think about adapting your style when you find yourself in a situation it doesn't suit.

This is one of the main reasons why people lack confidence and self-belief – they don't know when or how to adapt their communication style.

What is *your* natural way of communicating?

Before you can work out how to adapt your style, you need to establish what type of style you have. You need to know if it's helping you or hindering you in relation to your self-confidence. We're going to look at this in more detail now.

Most people think 'communication' is merely about talking. It's not though; talking is just one element of what it means to communicate. Try thinking more widely now about the concept of communication. For example, have you ever considered that *how* you say something might be just as important as *what* you say?

There are numerous models and theories that can help to identify your personal communication style. *Brilliant Confidence* keeps it simple and considers four different types of style. Each of these has its own traits and typical communication behaviours.

The four *Brilliant Confidence* communication styles are:

● Methodical

● Sensitive

● Up-front

● Animated.

Some people find that they see the traits of just one of these styles very strongly in themselves. Others find that they lean towards two of the styles. Others find that they don't have a particular leaning and have a balance of all four styles in their personal communication behaviour.

The aim here isn't to pigeon-hole you into one particular style but more to open your mind to the different ways people communicate. This should help you to have the confidence to use one of the styles you don't naturally lean towards when you're dealing with certain people.

Regardless of the style you naturally tend to adopt, it's important to understand that there is no 'best' or 'worst' style; there's no 'right' or 'wrong' style to have. However, there is an 'appropriate' style for certain situations. So, being able to adapt your style is pivotal if you want to come across as more confident and become more influential.

> there is no 'best' or 'worst' style; there's no 'right' or 'wrong' style to have

In Chapter 3 (page 68) you wrote down two lists when you were establishing your perception of yourself, one with positive descriptive words and the other with negative words. You might find it helpful to refer to it here. It should help you to identify your natural style.

The Think Confidence Communication Style Questionnaire

If possible you now need to visit the Think Confidence website (www.thinkconfidence.com) to complete your free Think Confidence Communication Style Questionnaire. This relates directly to the chart shown in Figure 4.1 and will help you to build a clearer picture of your natural communication style. The higher your points score for a particular style in the questionnaire, the more strongly you demonstrate the traits of that style in your natural communication behaviour. A high score would be considered as 11 or above.

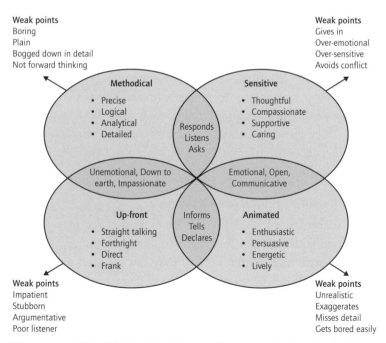

Figure 4.1 The Think Confidence Communication Style Chart

If you don't have internet access, don't worry; just look at the chart and try to work out where your natural style fits best. You know yourself better than anyone so you should be able to be pretty accurate.

The chart shows four style sectors: methodical, sensitive, animated and up-front. The strengths of each style are bulleted within its sector. On the outside of the chart, the weak points of each style are shown.

Let's look at the strengths and possible weaknesses of each style in a little more detail. While reading this, you're interested as much in the style(s) you score high in as you are the one(s) you score low in. That's because confident people have the ability to adopt the right style for the right situation. If you score low in a style, you'll need to start to learn how to use it because, at some point, it will be the style that suits best. We'll cover how you go about deciding this later.

Up-front style

Strengths
High scorers will look you in the eye and tell you what they think. They'll speak up forcefully when they have a point to make. They are decisive, will probably have a firm handshake and will walk with purpose. They like to get to the point, act and then move on.

Traits to watch out for (weak points)
High scorers think and talk in black-and-white terms. They may seem rude and too forthright to some people (particularly sensitive-style high scorers). They may fail to listen and to take account of other people's points of view. They could be prone to im-patience, be argumentative and ignore advice.

Animated style

Strengths

High scorers tend to be enthusiastic people who have a lively character. They like to talk, can be quite persuasive and are interesting to listen to. They have an energetic way about them and, if very high scorers, are often the 'life and soul of the party'.

Traits to watch out for (weak points)

High scorers can sometimes get carried away with themselves in terms of their thoughts and their excited behaviour. They think in terms of generalities rather than detail and practicality. This can mean that they exaggerate and that their ideas may verge on the unrealistic. They may also appear overdramatic, particularly to methodical people, who tend to be more down to earth in their approach.

Sensitive style

Strengths

High scorers have a genuine interest in others. They communicate this through their words and through their receptive body language. They are good listeners and have a considerate nature. They are often softly spoken and patient and will express their feelings freely. They value strong work and personal relationships.

Traits to watch out for (weak points)

High scorers tend not to like conflict. They'll try to avoid conflict in the hope that it will go away without them having to deal with it. They might even give in rather than let the conflict continue. When they feel strongly about something, they can be quite emotional and show their feelings very expressively. They can get distracted quite easily if conflict arises within a working relationship.

Methodical style

Strengths
High scorers like detail and order. They tend to be analytical and precise in the way they think and speak. They like to base their opinions on facts and practicalities rather than concepts. They may be quiet in character but when they speak they're normally worth listening to because they've thought carefully about what they're going to say.

Traits to watch out for (weak points)
High scorers have a tendency to get bogged down in detail and lose sight of the longer-term perspective. They tend to think on a day-to-day basis rather than strategically. They don't display much emotion and aren't very expressive. They can appear to some people (particularly animated-style high scorers) as boring or disinterested whereas, in fact, they are neither.

Overlaps

You'll also see on the Communication Style Chart that there are areas of overlap between style sectors. These show the behaviours that are common to both styles.

Methodical/Sensitive
If you score mainly across the top of the chart, in the methodical and sensitive sectors, your tendency is to want to listen, ask and then respond. In other words, you prefer to wait for the other person to speak before you do. You might even describe yourself as shy if your scores are high.

Up-front/animated
If your scores orientate towards the bottom two sectors of the chart, your tendency is to talk rather than to listen. In fact, if your scores here are high, you probably don't listen much at all. Your natural inclination is to deliver your opinion before hearing what others have to say.

Sensitive/animated

Scoring to the right of the chart suggests you are open in the way you communicate. It's probably quite easy for others to tell how you're feeling because you don't mind expressing your emotions. If you score very high in these sectors, you probably find your emotions getting the better of you on occasions.

Methodical/up-front

Scoring to the left of the chart suggests you prefer to keep your cards close to your chest. You tend not to be emotional and can perhaps be difficult to read. It's not that easy for others to tell what you're thinking or how you're feeling because you don't give much away through your body language or in terms of what you say.

Using the Think Confidence Communication Style Questionnaire effectively

Completing the Communication Style Questionnaire is an important step forward in your Confidence Project. You should feel more confident now that you know your strengths and you should feel in a stronger position to address your weaknesses. However, there's much more than just this to be gained from this knowledge.

To *really* use your natural communication style effectively, you'll need to open your mind a touch. People tend to be most comfortable talking to or working with people who have a similar communication style to them. That's because people who communicate like you behave in a way that you can relate to. They do the things you do and don't distract you or frustrate you by communicating in a way that you don't like.

The problems tend to arise when you're dealing with someone who has a different style to you. You've probably heard the phrase 'personality clash' many times – what people often actually mean is 'communication style clash'. Understanding your natural communication style is the first step to dealing with this.

You should by now have either completed the Communication Style Questionnaire or had a good look at the Communication Style Chart to discover your own style. Now you can think constructively about when and how to adapt it so that you can come across confidently and assertively.

Style clashes

The degree to which your style might clash with someone else's tends to depend on how strongly you portray that style. For example, it wouldn't be at all surprising if a high-scoring methodical-style person sometimes feels uncomfortable interacting with a high-scoring up-front person. This is because methodical people like detail, they like to consider the whole picture, they tend to listen before speaking, they're not very expressive and they would prefer to take their time to check things. Up-front people are very different; they are more forthright, they speak before listening or asking, they can be impatient, they get bored with detail and they tend to be louder and more imposing.

This is just one example of a style clash. There are many more, depending on the styles involved. When you look at the differences between the styles on the Communication Style Chart, it's not difficult to see the reasons why styles clash if neither person makes any effort to adapt.

So, having established your natural communication style, you're in a stronger position to use this knowledge to come across more confidently. Try to start thinking along the following lines:

- Be prepared to adapt your style when you're talking to someone.
- You're not 'giving in' when you decide to adapt; you're being clever.

- Don't *expect* the other person to adapt – they may have no knowledge of the communication style concept, so don't blame them.

Approach every situation positively and take it upon yourself to solve it.

Adapting and mirroring

'If you talk to a man in a language he understands, that goes to his head. If you talk to him in his language, that goes to his heart.'

Nelson Mandela

'Adapting and mirroring' is a great way to solve a communication issue and build rapport with other people quickly. It's a simple concept which involves watching, adapting to and then mirroring the other person's style and behaviour. It's absolutely true that the more you can mirror their communication style, the more comfortable they will feel in your presence.

To make this work, you'll need to increase your state of awareness. You'll need to be more observant when you're talking to people. You're trying to take in as much as you can, as quickly as you can, about their verbal and non-verbal behaviour. You're looking at the other person's body language, facial expressions, tone, pace, volume of voice, energy level, enthusiasm, expressiveness and emotion.

> you'll need to be more observant when you're talking to people

In fact, what you're doing is trying to identify their communication style. Ideally, you'll be able to gauge roughly where you think the person would fall on the Communication Style Chart. Once you've worked this out, you can start to think about how similar, or perhaps different, their style is to your natural style. The more different they are, the more you'll need to adapt.

Of course, there will be some people who have a similar style to you. You probably won't have to adapt a great deal, perhaps even at all, to mirror these people. It's the people who have different styles to you that you'll need to work hardest on. Don't forget the Communication Style Questionnaire when you're thinking this through. If you judge that the other person would score high in the questionnaire in a different style to you, the 'clash' could be quite significant. This could be even more pronounced if you yourself score low in their style.

So, when using the Communication Chart concept to feel and look more confident, your senses have to detect when you're dealing with someone who has a strong natural communication style that's different to yours. Be prepared for this and bear in mind that you'll find it harder to mirror the other person's style if you personally don't like it, feel comfortable with it or use it naturally. Bear in mind also that the higher you score in your own style, the more unnatural it will feel to mirror someone who is different to you.

brilliant tip

Be careful how you do this: I'm not talking about mimicking the other person's behaviour – you've gone way too far if you do this and you'll start to look silly. Mirroring behaviour has to be done subtly for it to be effective.

To give you a better feel for how to put the concept of adapting your style in practice, here are some examples of people who have employed it successfully.

brilliant example

Gethin

Gethin completed the Communication Style Questionnaire. His results showed the following scores for the four communication sectors:

- Methodical – 7
- Sensitive – 13
- Up-front – 4
- Animated – 4

This proved to be a useful exercise for Gethin. He began to realise why he didn't feel comfortable with certain people. There was one person in particular who he struggled with. When he thought about it, he came to the conclusion that this person (Aisha) probably scored high in the up-front sector on the chart. Whereas Gethin (sensitive sector score 13) was a caring person who was prepared to listen and take account of Aisha's thoughts and concerns, Aisha was a forthright, loud and, in Gethin's eyes, formidable person who didn't listen or show any interest in his point of view.

Gethin made a conscious decision to adapt in order to mirror Aisha's style the next time they met. Whereas before he had let her dominate the conversation, this time he looked her in the eye, spoke louder than normal, didn't waffle and explained his thoughts clearly and concisely. Having scored 13 in the sensitive sector, Gethin didn't find this easy to do because adapting meant behaving very differently to his natural preferred style. It worked brilliantly for him though.

He walked away from the meeting feeling that he had achieved what he wanted. Subsequently, with his new-found confidence, Gethin was able to talk openly to Aisha about how he had found the Communication Style Chart concept useful in terms of his working relationship with her. He was surprised to hear that she actually preferred him to be more up-front and found it easier to work with people like that! It was lucky she told him because, up to then, he'd thought that being so forthright with someone would surely sound rude or aggressive.

Gethin's decision to adapt to the up-front style worked well when dealing with Aisha. It wouldn't work though if he used it for someone who scored high in one of the other three styles.

> ### ☀ brilliant tip
>
> Remember to keep an open mind when using the Communication Style Chart concept. What works for one person might not work for another.

► brilliant example

Ellen

Ellen completed the Communication Style Questionnaire and scored as follows:

- Methodical – 5
- Sensitive – 6
- Up-front – 5
- Animated – 12

It had puzzled her why some people just didn't seem to take her seriously. It had never occurred to her that it might be something to do with her natural style. Ellen was a very expressive person who liked talking and tended to exaggerate. She liked to talk about ideas and got bored easily with any discussion that involved day-to-day practicalities.

She was so lively and enthusiastic about everything that some people found this completely over the top and unbearable. Ellen found this confusing because she thought these were positive traits. She even thought to herself on occasions, 'If everyone was as fun and lively as me, the world would be such a great place – some people are just so boring'.

▶

Ellen thought about her friends and work colleagues and tried to place each one of them in the Communication Style Chart. She started to see that the people she got on best with were the people who fell in the animated sector; in other words, she got on best with people who thought, talked and approached life like she did.

What she also started to see was that the people she clashed with tended to be the opposite to her. For example, she found one person (Susie) incredibly frustrating because she never showed any emotion. Susie always had the same expression and never seemed to get excited about anything – even good things. It got to the point where Ellen couldn't help seeing Susie as a negative person. What's more, Susie seemed paranoid about detail – everything had to be organised and in the right place.

Ellen was pretty certain that Susie would score high as a methodical-style person on the chart, the direct opposite to her own style. So she started to think about what she might need to do to mirror Susie's style. Thinking this through made her realise that, actually, Susie wasn't a negative person, she just communicated and behaved differently to her. Although it was a huge effort (because her own style was so strong and so different to Susie's), Ellen vowed that she would try to mirror Susie's methodical-style when she was dealing with her in future.

She did this by trying to control her emotion and to temper her loud and lively approach when she was with Susie. She also made a conscious effort not to get carried away with her ideas and to forget to ask and then listen to Susie's thoughts. She had to remind herself to have a structure to what she was saying so that Susie didn't think she was waffling. This helped her to cover the level of detail that Susie liked.

These simple changes in the way Ellen behaved made a huge difference, not just for her relationship with Susie but also for her self-confidence. She noticed that the people who used not to take her seriously started to ask her opinion more and listen more attentively to what she was saying.

Whereas Gethin found it helpful to project himself and talk more, Ellen found that she needed to temper her desire to speak and to try to listen more. Decisions like these can only be made by weighing up the differences between your style and the styles of the people around you.

brilliant tip

Keep an open mind and treat each person as an individual when deciding which style best suits.

brilliant example

Matt

Matt scored as follows in the Communications Style Questionnaire:

- Methodical – 7
- Sensitive – 7
- Up-front – 7
- Animated – 7

Matt's scores were balanced throughout the sectors. My experience is that Matt falls into a small minority of people who don't have a leaning towards one or two of the styles. In some ways Matt is lucky because he doesn't have to make the adjustment others need to make in order to mirror someone else's style. After all, having the same score throughout indicates that Matt naturally portrays all the styles in a measured way.

However, he shouldn't be complacent; he still needs to consider the styles of people around him. Just like everyone else, he needs to identify the style he needs to mirror. Just being his normal self might not be enough if the other person strongly displays the traits of a particular style. He'll need to adapt so that his style matches the strength of the other person's.

brilliant tip

If you complete the Communication Style Questionnaire and find your scores are fairly balanced, you'll still need to have the awareness and confidence to pick which style best suits the situation.

PART 3

Confidence in action

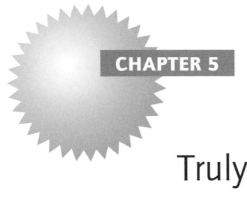

CHAPTER 5

Truly assertive communication

To be assertive is to influence

It's time to start thinking about putting your Confidence Project into action. Part three of *Brilliant Confidence* bridges the gap between thinking about being more confident and actually putting it into practice.

You'll see that the concept of *assertiveness* is a major component here. Some people find it hard to differentiate between assertiveness and confidence so let's clarify this straight away. We established at the beginning of *Brilliant Confidence* that confidence is a skill that relates to your attitude and your state of mind. Assertiveness is a skill too, but it relates to your behaviour rather than to your mindset. So, in short, confidence is a mental state and assertiveness is a behaviour. The important thing to acknowledge is that both are *skills* you can learn.

> confidence is a mental state and assertiveness is a behaviour

There's one major thing to remember here – self-belief and confidence *cannot* exist if you don't have the skills to be assertive. It's *that* important.

Confident people use assertive behaviour to influence others. *Influence* is having the power to affect someone's beliefs, actions or thought processes.

The chain is simple (see Figure 5.1).

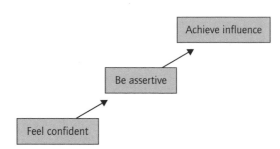

Figure 5.1 The influence chain

Finding a balance

Truly assertive people have found that critical balance between stating their case and taking account of the views of the other person. They've acknowledged that their own needs, wants and rights are equally as important as the other person's. Truly confident people have the ability to be truly assertive. They aren't just able to present their own case, they also have the sensitivity and moral courage to accommodate the other person's case if necessary. They might even give in if they think the other person is right or has a better idea.

True assertiveness falls in the middle of two extremes. It keeps the seesaw balanced (See figure 5.2).

People who use their self-confidence effectively are able to fine-tune the balance of the seesaw. They understand that both passive and assertive behaviour are required for true

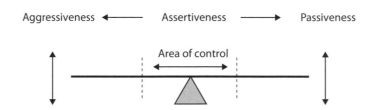

Figure 5.2 The assertiveness seesaw

assertiveness. However, they also know that extreme behaviour in one or the other direction can unbalance the seesaw to such an extent that control is lost. Confidence levels can be severely dented if this happens.

Let's have a look at what extreme behaviour in either direction constitutes.

Aggressiveness

Aggressive people boldly insist that their rights, views and needs prevail.

They fall into two categories:

● Those who have an inflated ego and an unrealistic sense of self-importance.

● Those who use 'aggressiveness' as a way of hiding a deeper sense of insecurity or another weakness.

Whichever category they fall into, aggressive people express their feelings and opinions in a way that violates the rights of others. They have no consideration for other's opinions and, in extreme cases, will be verbally and/or physically abusive in order to get their way.

Aggressive people may get away with it in the short term but eventually their behaviour will have a negative impact on their self-confidence and self-belief.

---

brilliant example

Pauline

Pauline was a newly qualified teacher in a secondary school. She had just finished her first year there. She was told by her department head during her annual appraisal that she was perceived by both colleagues and students as 'aggressive'. She'd known for a while that something wasn't ▶

quite right with her approach and manner but she hadn't been able to put her finger on it. It wasn't until her boss explained it that she realised. Pauline thought she was being 'confident', not aggressive. She thought that it was part of a teacher's job to behave like that.

We talked about this during the confidence-building course she attended. It soon became clear to her that her behaviour was weighing down the aggressive side of the seesaw; the passive side was way out of reach and almost in the clouds. She was strong at putting her point of view across but couldn't see that others were feeling threatened by her behaviour. The pupils were scared to ask questions and her colleagues felt uncomfortable working with her.

She started to see that she was shutting out other people's views and needs. She had genuinely thought she was an assertive person when, in fact, she was aggressive. She left the course with the aim of developing her passive side and her listening skills.

Pauline found the 'Turning the clock back' exercise (Chapter 1) very useful. She recalled a number of experiences she had had. These experiences had led her to feel insecure and uncertain of herself. Her aggressive behaviour was actually a 'smoke screen' that she deployed to hide these hidden vulnerabilities. She'd become very adept at this, so good in fact that no one had any idea she was acting. So, aggression wasn't her natural behaviour at all; when she relaxed and we got to know her better, we started to see her passive side coming out.

Understanding the need to find the middle ground to achieve true assertiveness was a major step forward for Pauline. Whereas before she'd felt that revealing her passive side would make her more vulnerable, during the course she started to see that showing your passive side is a critical part of feeling and being confident.

So, ask yourself if any of the following words describe the way *you* behave or treat people:

Humiliate, dominate, criticise, blame, threaten, interrupt, order, shout, bully ...

These are aggressive, not assertive behaviours. Don't be mistaken by thinking they are confident behaviours – they might seem confident in the simplest of physical senses but actually they'll work against you and hinder your self-belief and self-confidence eventually. You can't get away with behaving in this way for ever. People just won't accept it.

Passive-aggressiveness

Passive-aggressive people get their way by subtle, underhand means.

This is a style of aggressiveness that a very small minority of people demonstrate. As the name suggests, passive-aggressive behaviour is a style that mixes passiveness with aggressiveness. People appear passive on the surface but have an aggressive streak in their character. This aggressiveness isn't seen physically in the person's behaviour; they will strive to get what they want through subtle, indirect and hidden means. They will smile and look cooperative, but behind this veil they'll be plotting and scheming to get their way.

This behaviour goes completely against the concept of assertiveness because it is not *open*. Assertive people create a two-way dialogue which takes both people's viewpoints, feelings and needs into consideration. People who act in a passive-aggressive way tend to behave as they do because they feel incapable of dealing directly with people.

Passive-aggressive people will use facial expressions that don't match how they feel, they'll smile when they are angry, they are often sarcastic and they'll deny there's a problem when they know there is one.

Passiveness

Passive people don't express their own views and concede that other people's rights, views and needs prevail over theirs.

Passive people fall into two categories:

● Those who are too shy to voice their own opinions and needs.

● Those who are so 'nice' that they genuinely feel that other people's opinions and needs should prevail over theirs.

Whichever category they fall into, passive people avoid expressing their opinions or feelings, protecting their rights, and identifying and meeting their own needs. Passive people are the most likely to lack self-confidence in the obvious sense; they try to avoid the limelight and will often use their passive traits to achieve this. At the extreme, passive people give in and accommodate to such an extent that their opinions and needs are never heard, let alone considered.

brilliant example

Steve

Steve attended a confidence-building course run in the training room at his office. I remember him well. He walked in quietly and sat down without saying a word, even though some others had already arrived and were in conversation.

The course started and a pattern started to develop. Steve would only speak when prompted and struggled to say anything meaningful whenever it involved giving his opinion. He even found it hard to commit himself when asked what time would suit him best for lunch. His first reaction to this question was to listen to what time would suit the other people. As a result, we had lunch at a time that was convenient for them, not him.

It transpired during the afternoon that Steve had missed an opportunity due to his passive approach. He'd known at the beginning of the day that a new client was visiting to meet his boss at 12.30. His boss had even said that it would be great if Steve could find the time to introduce himself.

So, even when the opportunity presented itself, Steve failed to speak up. If he'd said something, we could have arranged the lunch break to accommodate him (particularly as no one else had any reason to ask for a specific time!).

Steve was demonstrating typically passive behaviour. His first thoughts focused on other people's opinions and wants rather than his own. Steve was a thoroughly nice person but was making the mistake of thinking that he would 'hurt people's feelings' if he told them what he thought or what he wanted.

So, ask yourself if you do any of the following:

- give in easily
- struggle to communicate your needs and wants
- allow others to influence you when you know you're right
- fail to express how you feel
- speak quietly or apologetically
- feel shy and try to avoid being in the limelight
- think so much about others that your needs suffer
- do other people's work before your own
- say 'yes' *every time* someone asks you to do something for them.

If you find yourself falling into these traps, you're definitely being too passive.

Don't worry about putting your point of view across and standing up for yourself. As long as you present yourself politely and take account of what the other person is saying (and accommodate if appropriate), your request should be received in a positive way.

Assertiveness

Confident people manage to find the middle ground between aggressive and passive behaviour. That's because they are in *assertive territory* (see Figure 5.3).

Assertive people clearly express and take into account that both people have rights, views and needs. Assertive people are comfortable stating their case while at the same time being respectful of the viewpoint of others.

The term 'assertiveness' can sometimes be misunderstood. It's helpful to set aside some misconceptions before we move on. Let's just clarify what assertiveness is *not*.

Assertiveness is *not* about:

● trying to dominate
● being louder than others
● being popular
● taking charge.

Assertive people have the confidence and the skills to influence others. They achieve this in an open, polite, sensitive but

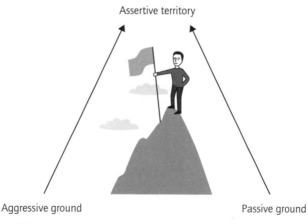

Figure 5.3 Assertive territory

authoritative way. They have found the right balance between passive behaviour (satisfying other's needs, wants and rights) and aggressive behaviour (demanding your own needs, wants and rights).

True assertiveness comes through confident, clear, calm and honest communication. Assertive people have the self-confidence to establish relationships in which everyone knows where they stand and everyone feels they have a say.

> true assertiveness comes through confident, clear, calm and honest communication

Balancing the bar

Have a look at the assertiveness seesaw below. Try to gauge where you think you fall on the bar. It's a simple but important exercise.

You might find it helpful to refer back to the two lists of adjectives you used to describe yourself in Chapter 3. Reflect again on the lists. It could be that a passive or aggressive theme emerges for you.

Put a cross where you think you fall on the line in Figure 5.4.

There are a number of reasons why the seesaw tilts. A serious tilt can lead to a loss of control.

I find that a lot of people who attend our confidence-building courses find themselves leaning towards the passive side of the

Aggressiveness ←——— Assertiveness ———→ Passiveness

Figure 5.4 The assertiveness seesaw model

seesaw. The interesting thing is that the majority of these people already know this. They also know that there are times when they need to be more direct and forthright in putting their point of view across. They just struggle to actually *do* it.

So, if you see yourself as passive, the first thing to accept is that *there is nothing wrong with being passive* – confident people can be passive but not to the extreme and not all the time. They know when a situation demands passive behaviour and will act passively to accommodate it. So don't fall into the trap of thinking your confidence levels are suffering because you're too 'nice' and 'accommodating'. You should be pleased you have this sensitive side to you – some people really struggle to find it.

I also find that very few people score themselves towards the left of the bar as aggressive. This doesn't necessarily mean I don't meet aggressive people though. It's just that aggression is often a characteristic that people can't see in themselves – they need to be told by others. The perception exercises you did in Chapter 3 might have helped you here.

The trick is to make sure the seesaw doesn't over-balance. If you lean too much towards the aggressive side, you need to temper your behaviour so that people don't feel threatened by it. If you lean too much towards the passive side, you'll need to develop the confidence to stand up for yourself when appropriate.

So how do you find this critical balance? You've already taken the first step by identifying where your natural behaviour positions you on the seesaw. The degree to which you lean one way or the other will dictate how far you need to move to be truly assertive. You might even find that you are already fairly central on the bar. That doesn't necessarily mean that you have nothing more to do though. You've still got to physically demonstrate assertive behaviour and that means *engaging* people.

Assertive behaviour – the thinking side

Truly confident people have overcome any possible hurdles in their mindset that may hinder their ability to be assertive. We know from Chapter 2 that confident people always think positively. They also continually remind themselves that *they have as much right* as anyone else to speak. If you're a passive person, you'll need to work hard at this.

People often come up with negative comments such as those listed below when explaining why they struggle to be assertive. Let's deal with these straight away.

Here are some typical comments to the question: 'I don't like the idea of being assertive because ...'

- *'People won't respect me'* – This couldn't be further from the truth. Try to think of people you know who speak their mind assertively. Do you disrespect them? I'd be very surprised if your answer is 'Yes'. My experience is that people have *more* not less respect for those who stand up for themselves and voice their opinion (as long as their message is presented politely). This is because you know where you stand with people who speak their mind.

- *'People will think I'm a negative person'* – They won't think you're a negative person as long as you use positive language to explain your position. Don't whinge, complain or criticise negatively. Don't make any presumptions regarding the assimilation of your message. Remember Chapter 3 and the lessons learnt about misinterpretation. If people know clearly the reasoning behind your point of view and the positives that may come from it, they shouldn't see you as a negative person.

- *'People will think I'm selfish'* – No one will think you're selfish if you show that you care. Yes, put your point of view across, but don't forget to show your passive side. People need to feel that you respect their opinion. To do this you have to let them share their thoughts with you. You also have to listen (we'll look in more detail at this later). Assertive people also keep an open mind – it could be that the other person says something that changes your opinion.

● *'People will think I'm a bully'* – They won't see you as a bully if you share your thoughts professionally and politely. Only aggressive people are seen as bullies. Your body language and physical presence make a massive difference here. We'll cover this in detail later in the chapter.

● *'People will dislike me'* – As long as you present your thoughts in a considered, sensitive and honest way (and not aggressively), most people would prefer to hear them than not. This is true even when they may disagree with you. They prefer to know what you're thinking rather than suspect that you're harbouring misgivings or not telling them something. They're more likely to dislike you for this than they are for presenting your thoughts to them confidently.

brilliant tip

Now that these demons have been set aside, don't forget – true assertiveness *requires* you to share your wants, needs and concerns. Assertive people know this and use it effectively to influence others.

Preparation

'One important key to success is self-confidence. An important key to self-confidence is preparation.'

Arthur Ashe, Wimbledon Men's Champion, 1975

Preparation requires time. Making time for yourself to prepare means being organised. We covered this to some extent in Chapter 3, so you'll know how being organised can boost your confidence levels. It's easier to make time to prepare for planned events like meetings, social gatherings or presentations than it is for unforeseen events. The difference here is that for planned events the time is already available whereas for unforeseen requests you may have to *make the time available* to think about your answer.

Preparing a confident answer to an unforeseen request

Some people are very good at pressurising you into doing things that you hadn't planned to do. They expect you to give them an answer there and then – they know what they want and they'll pile on the pressure to get it. *Don't let them get away with it.* The majority of requests made of you will not be affected if you delay your answer for a few minutes. Very rarely does a request require an answer there and then.

> very rarely does a request require an answer there and then

There are very few situations when it isn't possible to create this little window of opportunity to prepare your answer. Confident people are good at giving themselves time to think before they speak or act. This is vital if you're to come across assertively and credibly. If you have your wits about you, there *are* ways of creating time to prepare your answer *even* when someone approaches you and expects an answer immediately. If you can win a minute or two, that's potentially all you need.

So, how do you make this window of time available and how can you best use that time?

Be alert at all times. Be ready for people who make requests or demands of you. If it's a work situation, you may already know people who continually ambush you and ask you to do things. They're not going to suddenly stop doing this for no reason – so, if you know it's going to happen at some stage during the day, get ready for it. Have a reply prepared for the next time it happens. This will give you thinking time and should stop you giving a 'knee jerk' reply that you regret later.

Imagine then that I'm your boss and I stop you in the corridor. It's a busy day and you've got lots on your plate already. Out of the blue, I try to give you another job to be completed that day. What would your normal reply be? People who lack self-confidence tend to say 'Yes' and accept the task immediately; they don't want to let their boss down, be seen as negative, uncooperative, lacking motivation ... and the list goes on.

Of course, there's a good chance that having added this extra job to your list, one of *your* jobs that you'd planned to do doesn't get done. As your boss, I won't know this but may well find out later and blame *you* for being inefficient!

Deciding whether it's a 'Yes' or a 'No'

People who lack confidence find themselves continually under pressure because they accommodate others and say 'Yes' whenever a request is made of them. They might be lovely, helpful people but the bottom line is that they can be terribly inefficient simply because they just can't say 'No'. The difficulty is that once you're seen by others as a 'Yes' person, you become a magnet for them. They'll turn to you first when they need something done. You then end up doing other people's jobs, not your own.

↗ brilliant exercise

Yes or no?

Think of people you know who have the confidence to say 'No' when appropriate. The term 'when appropriate' is important here – you're thinking of people who have achieved the right balance, i.e. people who say 'Yes' when they think it's right to do so, but also have the confidence to say 'No' too.

Now ask yourself – would you describe any of these people you've thought of as negative, uncooperative or selfish just because on occasions they say 'No' to a request? I would guess not, because they've got the balance right. They'll accommodate and help when appropriate and have the confidence to say 'No' when necessary.

So, try to remember – there's nothing negative about saying 'No'.

It's easy to get into the habit of saying 'Yes' but, with practice, you can get out of it by taking some simple steps:

1. Don't give the person an answer there and then (it may not seem possible but this is possible in 99 per cent of situations – you need to try it to find out).

2. Tell the person you need a little bit of time to consider their request. Try to grab as much time as possible. Even a few seconds is better than nothing. An hour or longer is ideal (by then they might have found someone else to do the job anyway). Make sure you tell the person when you will give them an answer.

3. During the time you've bought yourself, consider the following:

● Is this a job I should be doing or is this person just trying to get me to do it because they don't want to do it themselves?

- If the request is work related, does it fall under my role and responsibility? (It's helpful to have an up-to-date job description, otherwise you might struggle to come to a balanced decision here).
- If I say 'Yes', how will doing this extra job affect my other priorities?
- If I say 'No', how am I going to tell the person this confidently and sensitively?

These steps should help you to make a balanced decision. You might only need a couple of minutes or less to do this for simple requests. For more complicated requests, try to buy as much time as possible.

Don't make the mistake of thinking that 'confident' people say 'No' all the time – they don't. If a 'Yes' is warranted and the knock-on effect to your own priorities is manageable, try to accommodate the person. Do this on *your* terms though. For example, if there's a degree of flexibility on timings, suggest that you will do the job when it suits *you*, not them.

The keys to saying 'No'

If a 'No' is warranted, there's an art to saying it. Don't go back to the person and simply blurt out 'No, I'm sorry I can't do that'. It might *sound* confident but it isn't clever. Believe it or not, there are ways of saying 'No' *positively*.

To achieve this, prepare your reply in three stages:

1. *Make a positive start* – Try to be sensitive and positive in your approach. i.e. '*I'd like to help* and I've thought carefully about your request but it's just not going to be possible this time because …'
2. *Explain the reasons why* – Don't make the assumption that the person knows why you've decided to say 'No'. Explain your reasoning, i.e. 'If I do this for you now, I'm going

to let other people down due to other deadlines I have to meet'. It might help to be more specific than this so that the person understands the reality of your predicament.

If you don't explain your reasons, there's a good chance you'll be perceived as being negative – after all, you can't expect the person to guess why you're saying 'No'. If it's a request from your boss, there's another benefit of explaining your reasons for saying 'No'; if your boss decides to override this and 'orders' you to do it, your boss now knows which deadlines you're going to miss as a result. You can't be criticised later for this because you clearly explained the implications of you doing it at the beginning.

On the other hand, your boss may well say 'OK, fine, don't worry then, I'll sort it out myself, I didn't realise how much you had on your plate'. If so, that's brilliant – you're in the clear!

3. *Suggest a possible solution* – Try to present the person with a possible solution that doesn't involve you. You might not be able to think of something every time but anything you can suggest that may help the person will be seen in a positive light, i.e. 'Have you thought about doing this/trying that/asking so-and-so ...?'

⌐ brilliant exercise

No magnets

Have a go. Try practising these approaches straight away. Make sure you're alert the next time someone requests something of you out of the blue. Most people find that it happens more often than they realised (particularly at work). You'll be amazed at how often you find yourself using these techniques. Be prepared though – when you start using them, it might seem like 'preparation overkill' for a reply to a simple request. It's not though – once you try it, you'll get the feel of it. Once you get practised at it, you'll see that you can come up ▶

with a balanced reply in just a few seconds. Eventually, for smaller requests, you should be able to give a prepared answer there and then. No longer will you find yourself giving 'knee jerk' answers which you subsequently regret.

Once you get into the habit of presenting your reasoning like this, people will start to see that the 'rules' have changed. No longer are you a 'Yes' person and therefore a magnet for people who are looking to spread their workload. As your colleagues, friends and relations get more and more used to this, they will change the way they treat you as a matter of course.

Here are some of the other benefits you can get from this simple concept of saying 'No' when appropriate:

● Your self-confidence starts to build.

● You can manage other people's requests rather than them managing you.

● You are seen to be a more confident person.

● You become more organised and better at managing your deadlines.

● People's respect for you grows because they know where they stand with you.

● You won't promise to do things that you then struggle to fulfil.

● You seize the initiative and take control.

● People only approach you when they have a relevant request.

● Your stress levels decrease because you're under less pressure.

● You end up doing your job rather than bits of everyone else's.

Preparing for a pre-arranged event

'The time to repair the roof is when the sun is shining.'

President John F. Kennedy

Preparing yourself in advance of the event is vital if you want to feel and look confident and in control when the event takes place.

Perhaps you've said 'Yes' to a request to give a presentation, play a part in a meeting or speak at a social engagement. Or maybe these types of events form part of your job or lifestyle anyway. Once more, good preparation could be the difference between success and failure. The better prepared you are, the more confident you will feel.

> the better prepared you are, the more confident you will feel

When you start your delivery on the day, you should already have a thorough knowledge of your message content and structure. People who feel and look confident when speaking have nailed this already. As a result they're able to focus their minds on the characteristics that confident people exude – charisma, enthusiasm, supportive body language and audience awareness.

With a pre-arranged event, you're in the lap of luxury of course with regard to preparation – whereas in the previous section you were preparing your answer to an unforeseen request and you only had a few minutes to decide whether your answer would be 'Yes' or 'No', now you've got time on your side.

So, whether or not you feel and look confident when the event takes place will depend very much on how well you prepare beforehand.

The 'W' concept

The following checklist is useful for all situations that involve you communicating information to others. They could be formal or informal situations at work or in your personal life – for example, meetings, presentations, social engagements, interviews and speeches.

Keeping your preparation method simple is essential. So ask

yourself these four simple questions *before* you start to prepare the actual content of what you're going to say.

Why?

What am I trying to achieve? What is my objective? If *you* don't know what you're trying to achieve, nor will the person (or people) you're talking to. If you tend to waffle, setting yourself a clear objective will keep you on track. As you move on to prepare what you're going to say, reflect regularly on your objective – continually ask yourself: does this help me to achieve my objective or is it just waffle?

When deciding on your objective, ask yourself what you're aiming to achieve:

- Am I trying to persuade?
- Am I trying to sell?
- Am I trying to inform?
- Am I trying to explain?
- Am I trying to amuse?

be crystal clear about what you want to achieve

Be crystal clear about what you want to achieve. Then tell the people right at the beginning what your objective is. Don't be frightened to do this. They will immediately perceive you as confident and in control if you state at the beginning what you aim to achieve (your body language must of course support this statement – we'll come to that later in the chapter). Everything you then say should relate to this objective and contribute in some way to its achievement.

Watch people sit up when you state your objective enthusiastically – it really works!

Who?

It's vital to do as much research as you can beforehand about who you're going to be talking to. You may know the people already but, even so, don't make any assumptions.

Ask yourself:

● Is it one person or a group (if so, how many)?
● What are their names, age bracket and backgrounds?
● If it's a work situation, what is the culture of their organisation?
● What do they need to know?
● What do they know already?
● What are their needs, concerns or sensitivities?

Confident speakers create a link with the person or group very quickly. They demonstrate an awareness that an audience might not necessarily *expect*. This is what sets a confident speaker apart from the rest. You can't do this if you haven't done any research. People respect speakers who show they've made an effort to learn about them; someone who cares and has their interests at heart.

> confident speakers create a link with the person or group very quickly

It's helpful to know how many people you'll be addressing. There are of course the obvious practical reasons for this – for example, the number of chairs, handouts etc. For me, though, the numbers are important for more subtle reasons. Knowing the number of people attending helps me to decide on my approach. I might run a meeting with a group of five or fewer people differently to a group of fifteen people – I might, for example, build in more 'discussion' time for the smaller group. In essence, I feel better prepared mentally if I know the group size beforehand – there are no 'shocks' in store.

Knowing their rough ages and a little about their backgrounds and experience can also help. For instance, you might consider dealing with a group of students differently to a group of directors.

Maintaining the group's interest and engaging them throughout is essential. You can only achieve this if you've thought about what they need to know, understood what they know already and considered their needs, concerns and sensitivities.

Finally, in the business context, researching the culture of the organisation and audience is also helpful. For example, you might choose to dress more smartly for one audience than another. This could make a real difference if, for example, you are a training consultant and looking to win a new training contract. The potential client will want you to fit in with their culture so that their delegates (i.e. the people you will be training) see you as credible and 'on their wavelength'; wearing a pinstripe suit to a meeting with a client in the arts field probably isn't going to send out the right message.

When?

This question is important in two respects:

- How much time is available for preparation?
- How much time is available for the delivery of your message?

If possible, give yourself more time than you think you'll need. I always try to have the preparation complete at least two days before the event. This may sound incredibly conservative and organised but it's worth the effort. It gives me time to reflect and relax while reviewing what I've prepared. I *always* change something to improve it or notice something that wasn't quite right. This extra little window of time helps to cement that feeling of confidence you need if your performance is to be excellent rather than just good. Don't let yourself down by having something go wrong that you could have sorted out if you'd prepared properly.

It's difficult to judge how much information you'll need to prepare if you're given a defined time slot for the event. The general rule is that you're better off with more rather than less. At least this way you won't finish early. I'd rather have the choice of leaving some points out and finishing on time than finishing early because I didn't have enough content. So, an element of your preparation should be determining which points are optional (and can be left out in the event that you're going too slowly) and which are not. Be careful though – you don't want to be leaving out essential points that help to achieve your objective.

It's very important that you get to the meeting room or venue first. Give yourself as much time as possible to set up. Always build in time for unforeseen occurrences (equipment failure, room change, someone introducing themselves to you beforehand and wanting to chat, etc).

Where?

Try to ensure the room and equipment layout suits *you*. You need to be 100 per cent focused on your delivery from the start rather than feeling uncomfortable and distracted because something isn't working or is in the wrong place. I never feel comfortable if I haven't actually seen the room beforehand. This isn't always possible though, so, as a second option, try to find out about it – there may be photographs available, etc.

The same principles apply to a formal presentation, where you might stand at the front, as to a meeting where you're sitting round a table. You need to know the answers to the following questions:

- How big is the room and how many people will it accommodate?
- What projection equipment is available?
- Is there natural daylight?
- How many tables and chairs are available?

- What is the situation regarding refreshments?
- How do you control the lights, the heating or the air conditioning?

You need to know where you will stand and set the room up in such a way that you can move around it if you need to. You *must* be able to have eye contact with every member of the audience throughout. Excellent speakers never forget this essential rule.

You shouldn't be too close to the closest members of the audience (you don't want them craning their necks or feeling uncomfortable) and yet you shouldn't be too far away either – the balance shouldn't be difficult to achieve but you might need to move chairs and tables around to find it. Believe me, it's worth thinking about this beforehand. There's nothing worse than realising too late that someone either can't see your screen, is sitting with a table leg in the way, or just doesn't look comfortable for some other reason.

confident people control the room

Confident people control the room. It's very difficult to do this if you haven't prepared it to suit you in advance. Set the room up so that you can *take centre stage*. Don't be a coward ... Resist the temptation to set the room up in such a way that the projection screen is the focus of attention. If you look as though you're trying to hide, you'll just draw more attention to yourself.

brilliant tip

Don't forget that you have to be seen to be seen to be confident.

Finding the answer to the question 'Where?' is just as applicable to a social event or engagement as it is to a presentation. If you're concerned about meeting new people or people you haven't seen socially for a long time, try to find out how the event is going to be run. Are you going to be sitting down (perhaps at a meal) and talking to one or two people for any length of time? If so, try to find out who they are! That way you can prepare better for the conversation. Or are you going to be mostly standing and mixing with different people? This gives you more flexibility because you can move around as you wish. You'll still need to prepare though – for example, you'll need to prepare for initiating a number of different conversations rather than just the handful that you would if you were sitting down.

How are you going to do it?
Having asked yourself the simple 'Why?', 'Who?', 'When?' and 'Where?' questions, you should be in a much stronger position to decide how best to go about your presentation preparation. In other words, how best to achieve your objective.

Try to keep an open mind here. It may well be easier to follow the crowd and do what others before you have done – perhaps use a template presentation that someone else has created or given. Watch out for your gremlin again here. Try to have the self-confidence to think outside the box – think about creating something of your own. You'll find it easier to come across more confidently if *you personally* create the message. You'll know it better and be more familiar with it. It's harder to communicate someone else's ideas confidently than it is your own.

So try to have the self-confidence to do something new, something different perhaps to what others might have done before. Confident people are prepared to accept this kind of challenge. It might involve more work and effort on your part but it's worth it. Having the courage to take a step into the unknown and to try something new will boost your self-confidence. The more you do this, the more confident and comfortable you'll feel. People around you will also start to see you as a more open-minded person who's prepared to try new ideas and to push the boundaries. These are all positive traits that confident people possess.

brilliant example

Nadia

Nadia worked for a children's charity and had recently been promoted to the position of marketing team leader. It was the first time she'd had any real responsibility for people. She now had a small team of five to manage.

Nadia attended one of our confidence-building courses. She was particularly interested in boosting her confidence when speaking in public. This was because she wanted to arrange a weekly meeting with her new team. She thought this would be a good idea because, in her words, 'the previous head of the team used to do it'.

The 'W' concept helped Nadia to open her mind. Just *thinking* about it made her feel more confident. She realised that having a weekly meeting just 'because the previous head of the team used to do it' was just plain daft! However, she knew that getting her team together on occasions was important because information did need to be communicated and discussed as a group.

So, having considered the 'W' concept she came up with a plan for her new weekly meetings:

 brilliant example

1. Why? – Meeting objectives:
- To ensure that information is communicated to the team on a timely basis.
- To provide the team with an opportunity to discuss problems and current issues.
- To provide the team with an opportunity to present ideas for more effective working.

2. Who? – Attendees:

- Five team members (two inexperienced, three experienced).
- Joe (sales manager) to attend on alternate weeks.

3. When? – Date and timings:

- 11 am on Monday (not 9 am as before because people always had issues to attend to first thing on a Monday).
- Meeting not to last longer than 1 hour (if further issues need discussing, another meeting should be arranged).

4. Where? – Location:

- In the Boardroom (not huddled round someone's desk in the office as before, where distractions continually interrupted).
- Allows for use of PowerPoint presentation software with laptop and projector.
- Sends message that meeting is important.

5. How? – What sort of shape will it take?

- Informal but more serious and better managed than previous meetings.
- Request that any issues people want to raise are sent out on previous Friday morning. Agenda sent out in afternoon.
- Meeting split as follows:
  - My part (my personal messages and communication of relevant company information – use PowerPoint when helpful).
  - General discussion of issues others wish to raise.
  - Any other issues or problems.
  - Agreement on actions for the week.

Using the 'W' concept made Nadia realise how bad the previous weekly meetings had been. She'd always felt that they were a bit of a waste of time but hadn't really thought seriously about why.

She now had a plan. Prior to thinking properly through the 'W' concept, she'd been very nervous about the meeting – mainly because she felt she lacked the confidence to run it properly. She wanted to start her new role well and felt that this meeting might threaten that.

She now had something concrete to guide her. In fact, once she'd finished her notes using the 'W' concept, she described her feelings: 'It was like having another person there by my side to support me'. The result was that her self-confidence started to rise. This helped her to feel in control right at the start and then throughout her first meeting. This set the precedent for future meetings because she immediately started to generate respect from her team.

brilliant tip

Have the discipline and patience to use the 'W' concept whenever you start your preparation for a pre-arranged event that involves communicating a message to an audience. It lends itself perfectly to preparing what you're going to say at a meeting, a presentation, a job interview or for a social speech.

What ifs

Try to predict the type of questions people might ask you. It's great when someone asks you a question that you've already thought about. You'll be able to answer a lot more confidently if this is the case. Put yourself in the place of your audience – ask yourself 'What would I ask if I were them?'

You might consider using the SWOT principle for this:

- Strengths – what are the strengths of my plan?
- Weaknesses – are there any weaknesses I've decided not to mention?
- Opportunities – what are the wider opportunities that may come from it?
- Threats – what are the threats to its success?

With a little forethought, using the SWOT principle, it's often possible to predict the types of questions you might be asked. That means you can prepare and rehearse some answers to questions that might come your way. Let's say you're presenting the monthly sales figures to your management team. The chances are your report will cover most of the obvious questions that the management team might have, but what other questions might you predict? What's different about this month? What new questions might be asked? How would you respond? What additional information might you need to have to hand to support more detailed questions?

In particular, spend some time brainstorming the most difficult questions that people might ask, then try to prepare, and if possible rehearse, good answers to them.

Can you think on your feet?

Giving yourself time is always going to help if someone puts you on the spot. However, the reality is that, on some occasions, no matter how hard you try, you have no choice but to answer there and then.

Self-confidence is key when learning to think on your feet. Your confidence will start to build if you follow some of these simple rules:

- *Knowledge* – If you're going to give a reply, make sure you know what you're talking about! That doesn't mean you have to be an expert, you just have to know enough to give a qualified answer. If you're reasonably confident in your knowledge of the subject, that confidence will help you to stay calm and in control even if you unexpectedly find yourself being put on the spot.

- *Never guess the answer* – If you don't know the answer, be honest and say so. Even experts in their field are stumped by a question sometimes. Don't try to make an answer up. There's a good chance you'll get caught out and this could seriously impact on your self-confidence later. Confidently explain that you don't know the answer and make sure you agree a time when you can contact the person subsequently to provide the answer.

Here are a few more simple things you can do to help you think on your feet. You can use these at all times, even when someone challenges you unexpectedly during the day.

- *Try to relax* – It's easy to say but perhaps not so easy to do. At least if you *try* to relax, you've got a chance. If you don't, you'll look and feel more stressed. You'll have more control of your voice, you'll feel calmer and you'll be able to think more clearly. Taking deep breaths while the person is asking you the question can also really help here.

- *Listen carefully* – Listening properly and attentively requires an effort. Some people forget this. You should be trying as hard when you're listening as you are when you're talking. It's obvious that you'll struggle to think on your feet if you aren't listening properly to the question. Don't interrupt the person – firstly because it's rude and secondly because, if you reply too soon, you may well give a wrong or inappropriate answer.

- *Ask the person to repeat the question* – This gives you those vital few seconds to think about your response. Try to be confident when you do this. Don't let your body language give away the fact that you're unsure of the answer. If your body language is positive and confident, the person will 'read' your request positively, i.e. they'll have the perception that you want to help by making sure you understand the question properly.

- *Repeat the question yourself (out loud)* – This gives you time to think and to clarify exactly what's being asked. Sometimes the person will reply and clarify their question after you've repeated it – that creates even more time for you. If you don't feel that the question is clear, have the confidence to ask for clarification. Again, if you do this confidently, it will be received positively because the person sees that you genuinely want to give a qualified answer.

- *Pause* – Don't be afraid to pause before you answer. People who lack confidence really struggle to cope with silence. They feel exposed and their natural defence is to fill it – normally without thinking about *how* they're filling it. Then, before they know it, they've said something they wished they hadn't.

- Confident people can use silence to their advantage. If you think about it, it's totally understandable that you should think about your answer before you give it, so a short silence shouldn't be unusual. If you look comfortable with silence and use it confidently, you'll send the message that you're in control of your thoughts and confident in your ability to answer. Critically, of course, you also create more time to think.

> confident people can use silence to their advantage

- *Don't waffle* – Once you understand the question clearly, make sure you stick to the point. Your answer should be specific and focused. If you're perceived as a waffler, the person may well start to lose interest – once *you* see this happening, your self-confidence is going to suffer.

When you've finished giving your answer, resist the temptation to add more information. There may well be a silence after you've finished. Don't make the common mistake of feeling the onus is on you to fill it with more information! You'll lose control of the conversation if your answer starts to drift.

> ### ☀ brilliant tip
>
> Don't jump in and give a knee-jerk reaction when someone puts
> you on the spot. Act calmly and take your time before you answer.
> There's nothing wrong with saying you don't know, as long as you
> go back to them with an answer later.

Nerves and anxiety

There will be times when you feel anxious, perhaps even worried
about putting some of these principles into practice. That's completely understandable – after all, you're doing things differently
to the way you're used to doing them, so they're not going to
come naturally.

> try not to see nerves as
> a negative thing

You're bound to feel a bit edgy about
this and as a result you may well get
nervous. The key is to try not to see
nerves as a negative thing.

Believe it or not, nerves are a good thing as long as you can
control them! Nerves give you adrenalin; if you can channel
it effectively, adrenalin can provide a fantastic boost to your
motivation, enthusiasm and confidence. Adrenalin gives you the
natural fuel you need to get you into the right gear to tackle the
situation. You don't even have to pay for it! Actors and public
speakers *all* feel anxious before they get on the stage (anyone
who tells you otherwise is more than likely being economical
with the truth). They know how to make this anxiety work in
their favour; they know how to channel it to help them enhance
their performance.

On the other hand, if you let your nerves get the better of you,
you'll get distracted, embarrassed and ultimately your self-confidence takes a nose-dive.

The tips on communication style and assertiveness in Chapters 3 and 4 will stand you in good stead here. They'll help you to overcome the physical signs of nerves that you might portray in your body language and voice. If you use these tips and keep practising, you'll find that you're able to channel your natural anxiety into positive energy that can actually help, not hinder you.

Assertive behaviour – the physical side

When you think about the way you communicate, you tend to think mainly about what you say. That's understandable because your voice is pivotal to sending a message. However, the reality is that only a small percentage of communication involves actual words. Studies conducted in the mid-1960s by Albert Mehrabian, Professor Emeritus of Psychology at the University of California, Los Angeles (UCLA), indicated that the impact of someone's performance is determined 7 per cent by the words used, 38 per cent by the voice quality and 55 per cent by the non-verbal communication used. Mehrabian's 7–38–55 rule is based on two studies reported in the 1967 papers 'Decoding of Inconsistent Communications' and 'Inference of Attitudes from Nonverbal Communication in Two Channels'.

 brilliant exercise

Look and learn

'Example is the school of mankind, and they will learn at no other.'

Edmund Burke, statesman, philosopher and author

The next time you're in a meeting or at a social event, look around the room. Watch how people conduct themselves. Try to set their voice apart from their body language and consider the two separately. Ask yourself who looks confident and who doesn't. Then think about why you've ▶

categorised people as confident or lacking confidence. Write down the things people are doing that make them look confident in your eyes. Who looks impressive and who doesn't? Why do some people look more alert than others? Why do you tend to listen to certain people but not others?

Look carefully. You're interested in how they behave – you're looking for the subtle things as well as the more obvious things. Look at how they sit, how they engage people, how they use their body to reinforce their message, what they do with their hands and eyes. You're looking for *anything* that makes them look confident. Very importantly, you're also looking for anything that suggests that they lack confidence.

Reflect now on the list you've made – try to split it between the way they talked and the way they used their body language. The behaviours that support a confident demeanour are just as important to identify as those that don't – you can learn a huge amount by just watching the way other people conduct themselves.

Don't forget – confidence is a skill you can learn. There are many professional sportsmen and women who will tell you they learnt the majority of their skills by *watching* professionals they admired and then copying them.

The next time you go to a meeting or a social event, reflect on the list you made above before you go in. You might even have it close by during the meeting. Do your best to replicate some of the confident behaviours you've identified in other people. Don't try to achieve them all straight away. Have a plan and focus on one or two each time. Don't move on until you're happy that the ones you've started with are working. This is a great way to boost your confidence – just by making some very subtle changes to your style, you'll be amazed at how people respond more positively to you.

Don't forget also to have the list of negative points you've identified nearby too. These of course are things you *don't* want to be doing. Regularly reflect on this list to make sure you're not slipping into any of those traps.

Verbal and non-verbal communication

Having completed the 'Look and learn' exercise, you've started to consider the concepts of 'verbal behaviour' and 'non-verbal behaviour'. You've probably heard the terms before but have you ever used them constructively in relation to the way *you* come across?

Well, that's exactly what we're going to do here. But first let's clarify what the two terms actually mean.

● Verbal communication = *What you say and how you say it.*

● Non-verbal communication = *What you do and how you do it.*

Verbal communication

What are you going to say?

Don't forget to use the 'W' concept if you can make the time. It will put you in a stronger position when you develop your thinking about what to say. In particular, you're using the answers to the 'Why?' and 'Who?' questions – they will help you to keep focused on your objectives and to have the interests of the person or people you're talking to in your mind at all times.

For situations like interviews, meetings, social speeches and presentations, you might also consider using the mind map process covered in Chapter 2 – it's a great way of setting out your thoughts quickly and creatively.

Structure

You'll feel more confident and in control if you deliver your message logically. The audience will also feel more comfortable because they'll find it easier to assimilate the information. The secret here is to keep it simple. If you're giving a presentation or a speech, keep it simple by having a clearly defined beginning, middle and end.

If you're preparing for a meeting, a well-thought-through agenda will help.

Credibility

To feel and look confident, you have to feel and sound credible. So what is 'credibility?' A listener sees you as 'credible' when they trust and believe your message. In relation to verbal communication, this means the content of your message must signal preparation, knowledge and relevance. In relation to non-verbal communication it means looking and sounding trustworthy, reliable, aware and in control (we'll come back to how you can help yourself to portray these characteristics later in the chapter).

> to feel and look confident, you have to feel and sound credible

You can blow your credibility very quickly even if you look and sound credible. If you promise to do something, make sure you do it – otherwise, the next time you speak to the person, even if you look and sound credible, they won't *believe you*. This is bound to have negative implications for your relationship with them and eventually your self-confidence will suffer.

brilliant tip

When you're preparing your message, be sure you mean what you say. If you promise to do something, make sure you can and will do it.

Confirmation

We tend to make the assumption that everyone interprets our message the same way. This just isn't true.

How often is it that you tell someone something and they get the wrong end of the stick? Don't worry, it happens to us all. It's not unusual for even the simplest of messages to be misunderstood. It's all down to misinterpretation; the other person has their own interpretation of your message. It's frustrating because, more often than not, the person *does* actually want to help. But, through no fault of their own, they go away with the wrong understanding. This can lead to all sorts of confusion; potentially they'll go away and do something different to what you asked, think something different to what you're thinking or perceive something wrong about your motivations.

You can normally tell by someone's facial expression if they're confused. Confident people don't just see this and accept it, they do something about it. They have the confidence to ask the person what their interpretation of the message is. In other words, they generate a dialogue which ensures *confirmation*.

If you stay aware, you should be able to work out when someone is confused about your message. The difficulty is that, quite often, a person won't tell you – because they're shy, they don't want to look stupid or they don't want to make it look as though they're criticising or questioning you. However, all is not lost if they don't actually verbally tell you they're confused. More often than not, the person will show through their *expression* that they need help understanding you. The person might not be physically talking and telling you this, but they're still communicating the message to you. Quite often they'll do this subconsciously. A confident person acknowledges this, tries to work out the meaning of the expression and does something about it. Basically, confident people don't have a problem asking if the person seems unsure about their message.

So, reacting to a confused expression is important in order to achieve clarity in interpretation. The real difficulty comes when the person genuinely thinks they have the right interpretation and goes away and does something different to what you were asking. *Don't make the mistake of blaming them straight away for this.* This tends to be what we do – after all, it *must* be their fault if they get the wrong end of the stick! People who think they understand you won't send confused messages through their expression because they're not confused! That's why it's so important to check the message has been received as you want it to be, *regardless* of their expression. This isn't difficult to do – the most difficult part is remembering to do it!

brilliant tip

Don't be too quick off the mark to blame someone for misinterpreting your message. You need to *look at yourself* first. It may be something to do with the way you're delivering the message. It may actually be your fault!

Paraverbal communication

To feel confident and to reduce the chance of misinterpretation, you have to be able to control the *way* you deliver your verbal message. This is sometimes referred to as the 'paraverbal' side of communication. There are huge advantages to be gained from getting this right but there are also significant dangers if you get it wrong. Confident people use paraverbal communication to their advantage. This gives them the power to control the way they present messages verbally.

You might find it helpful to refer back again to the 'Look and learn' exercise here. Did you identify any of the following characteristics during the exercise?

Speed of delivery

There is of course the obvious reason for not speaking too fast; people find it hard to assimilate your message and therefore to understand it. You just can't expect people to take it all in if you deliver the message at 100 mph. Watch out here because even if you don't naturally speak fast, if you're nervous, you might find yourself rushing. This is normally for one of two reasons:

● You're desperate to get out of the limelight as soon as humanly possible.

● You're naturally a fast speaker and you're not controlling the habit.

Most people know whether or not they speak fast. Perhaps this was mentioned in the feedback the person gave you when you tried the 'Straight talking' exercise in Chapter 3. If you're still not sure though, try to find out, because it can make a big difference.

Talking too quickly can make you look edgy or stressed. People who look confident just don't do this. They are able to overcome any urge to speed up. They speak at a measured pace that's comfortable for the other person or the audience. This helps them to look and feel in command. It also helps them to control their thought processes. The reason for this is simple – their brain can keep up with them!

> talking too quickly can make you look edgy or stressed

The pause

It might seem like simple advice, but using pauses as you speak is essential to coming across as confident. The difficulty is that a pause means a silence; even the shortest of silences can seem like an eternity when you're in the spotlight. This is one of the reasons why pausing can be so effective – if people are expecting you to say something and yet they see that you look comfortable with the silence, you can use it really effectively. I'm not talking about minutes of silence here, just a few seconds.

Be careful though – don't fall into the trap of filling the pause with noise. Noise feels better than silence when people are staring at you ... so you say 'umm'. People then start to perceive you as nervous and lacking confidence.

Most people think that the reason your voice sounds juddery when you're nervous is obvious – it's all to do with your mental state. What they don't realise is that actually, in pure physiological terms, nervousness in your voice comes about through physical, not psychological reasons. Therefore, if you think logically about it, if you know what to do, with practice you should be able to overcome saying 'umm' and therefore sounding nervous.

You can't afford to do *anything* that makes you look nervous. If you really think about it, saying 'umm' is just silly – it might make you feel better, but it definitely doesn't make you look better – why do it then?

> you can't afford to do *anything* that makes you look nervous

So how do you stop 'umming?' You'll be relieved to hear that it's really not that difficult.

↗ brilliant exercise

No more umms

Find a quiet place on your own. Then, say 'umm' a few times out loud. Now think about what you have to do physically with your breathing to say 'umm'. The answer is simple – you have to breathe out. That means you can't breathe *in* ... and that means you're starving yourself of air. It doesn't take long for your voice to be affected by this because all you can do is snatch shallow breaths as you talk. Soon, your voice starts to waver and break up. It gets worse and worse the longer you speak. The reason is simple – you just don't have enough air in your lungs to be able to project your voice with any strength. It then becomes a snowball effect – you start to hear yourself sounding nervous, you become more and more self-conscious about it and then other nervous traits start to kick in. Eventually your attention is drawn away from what you're saying and you lose control because you're getting hijacked by the state of your nerves.

So, if you want to stop 'umming' there are two essentials to remember:

● Discipline yourself to pause regularly as you speak.

● Make sure you breathe in while you pause.

Just to reinforce that this shouldn't be difficult to do: try saying 'umm' at the same time as breathing in. Have a go now – take a big breath in and say 'umm' while you're doing it. Point made? You can't do it, can you!

---

brilliant tip

It's essential to pause so that you can breathe regularly while you're speaking. If you don't breathe, you starve your lungs of air. This will severely hinder your chances of projecting your voice confidently.

Not only does pausing ensure you stop saying 'umm'. It also forces you into creating a silence. There are other major advantages too:

● You give yourself more time to think.

● You give yourself a chance to look at your notes and check what you're going to say next.

● You give yourself more time to watch the audience.

● You give the audience more time to take in your message.

● You look and sound in control.

● You give yourself those vital seconds you need to gather yourself when something has distracted you or you've lost your train of thought.

● You give yourself that vital time to breathe.

And of course ...

● You look confident – confident people don't have a problem with silence. In fact they use it to their advantage.

Varying the pace

Once you're happy with the speed at which you speak, you can start to think about varying it. If you listen to people who are confidently assertive, you'll hear them varying the pace of their delivery as they speak.

I find that it's really effective if you slow down slightly when you're voicing an important point. If you want to draw particular attention to something, say it slightly slower – you'll see people's heads bob up as you do it. This is simply because you're doing something different – you're varying the pace of your delivery. It's a simple idea but a great technique.

Be careful though – don't overdo it. If you do, your pace will be so varied that it will turn into a distraction. You could also be in danger of being perceived as patronising if you keep slowing down to make points. This technique is most effective if used sparingly and carefully.

Intonation

You've probably heard people who speak with little or no into-nation in their voice; they communicate verbally in a monotone way. I'd be surprised if you would describe any of these people as confident. You're probably more likely to use words like 'boring', 'disinterested', 'de-motivated' or 'shy' to describe them. In other words, speaking in a monotone has direct links to people's per-ception of your confidence.

People with good intonation are able to control the rise and fall of their voice. There are a number of advantages to doing this:

- You sound more interesting.
- You sound and look more interested in your subject.
- You look more relaxed and natural.
- You give a more positive impression.

If you use intonation effectively, you'll also find it easier to emphasise words. This is a great way of improving the clarity of your message. Have look at this sentence and read it to yourself;

> I didn't lose the letter she wrote to you.

Now read it again and emphasise the word highlighted each time:

> I didn't lose the letter she wrote to *you*.
> *I* didn't lose the letter she wrote to you.
> I didn't lose the letter *she* wrote to you.

You can see that the clarity (and perhaps even the meaning) of your message can change if you emphasise a different word each time. This could make quite a difference if you're trying to defend yourself against an accusation or if you want to make a specific point.

So, if you tend to speak in a monotone, start trying to modulate your tone. You'll be amazed at how people respond more positively to you. You'll also significantly reduce the chance of them misinterpreting your message.

Enthusiasm

This is infectious. If you sound enthusiastic, the people or person you're talking to will feel enthusiastic about what you're telling them. It works the other way too of course – if you sound unenthusiastic, your message won't be received positively.

Varying your tone can help with this; people will want to listen to you more if you generate enthusiasm in your voice. Of course, this isn't difficult if you're genuinely enthusiastic about what you're talking about. If so, hopefully you'll naturally sound enthusiastic. I say hopefully because it isn't a foregone conclusion that this will happen. Some people don't sound enthusiastic even when they're talking about something they're genuinely enthusiastic about.

I regularly invite people on confidence-building courses to tell us about the most interesting thing they've ever done in their life. It's amazing how some people do this. This is what happened when Scott told us about his *most interesting experience ever*.

---

brilliant example

Scott

Scott told us about an experience he'd had on holiday in South Africa. He'd gone on an organised trip to see great white sharks. He recounted in detail to us how he'd been lowered from the boat in a cage and how the sharks had swum around the cage. He told us how close they came, how they bumped the cage and even how he could 'see right down into the mouth of one of them past the razor-sharp rows of teeth'. He told us how terrifying it was and how he'd never forget it – ever …

But he told the whole story in a monotone voice with no emphasis at all. In other words, you would never have thought it was the most interesting thing he'd ever done. It got to the point where you started to wonder if he'd actually even enjoyed it, let alone considered it the most interesting thing he'd ever done.

If you struggle to sound enthusiastic about something you naturally feel enthusiastic about, imagine what's going to happen when you're telling people about something you're not naturally enthusiastic about!

This perhaps might be a situation at work; you might be talking about a work topic that's important but that you don't feel particularly interested in. In situations like that, you've got to make a major effort to pump yourself up so that you come across enthusiastically. If you don't, you'll sound disinterested yourself.

brilliant tip

Enthusiasm is infectious; it can work for you if you project it, but against you if you don't.

Non-verbal communication

There are two themes to consider here:

- Making sure your body language isn't a distraction.
- Using your body language to support and reinforce your message.

Distractions

Being aware of any unusual physical habits you have when you communicate is essential. The last thing you want to be doing is distracting the person while you're talking to them. You need to make it as easy as possible for them to take in your message. Just one small unusual habit could cause a distraction and blow your confidence out of the water.

Confident and truly assertive people have already worked out if they have any distracting habits. They've also worked out a strategy to overcome them. The 'Straight talking' and 'Self-perception' exercises in Chapter 3 will have helped you to identify any habits you have. We may have already touched on some of them, so you should already be in a stronger position to address them.

> confident and truly assertive people have already worked out if they have any distracting habits

Supportive body language

Imagine you're a soldier going into battle. On your belt, easily accessible, you have a number of essential pieces of equipment to keep you alive: ammunition, grenades, bayonet, medical kit, water and radio. At some point, you will need to use all these items if you're to survive and win.

You can draw a clear comparison here with confidence. Whereas the soldier is going into battle, you are living your life, your confident life. So, on *your* belt you have your own essential pieces of equipment available to support you: eyes, posture, walk, hands and facial expression. Just like the soldier, it's essential that you use all of these physical traits in order to win. Winning for you is looking and feeling confident. We all have our belt with the essential equipment on it. People who lack confidence tend to forget it's there.

So how can you make the most of the equipment on your belt?

Effective eye contact

It's amazing how people's perceptions can differ when they see a person not making eye contact when they're speaking to them. These perceptions do have one thing in common though – they are *all* negative. Here are some of the comments we get on our confidence building-courses about people who have poor eye contact:

'They don't believe in what they say.'
'They don't know what they're talking about.'
'They look shifty and untrustworthy.'
'They aren't interested in the audience.'
'They look nervous.'
And of course …
'They lack confidence.'

You can employ some simple techniques to improve your eye contact.

Have the confidence to take a moment to look at the person or people *just before you speak*. This sends the message that you're not frightened and you're in control. It's a great way of commanding immediate attention. Without even saying anything, you'll also send the message: 'I'm ready and I'm confident'. They'll see this and if there's a hubbub of general conversation going on, they'll soon stop. If possible, don't start talking until there's complete silence.

Look at people while you're speaking. If it's a small group, try to look at each person regularly. Try to find the balance: you shouldn't hold your eye contact for too long because you'll make the person feel uncomfortable. On the other hand, you do need to hold it for long enough to make 'contact'.

I rarely meet people who are naturally good at this. The majority have to work hard at it to get it right. It's worth it though because, once you've cracked it, you'll see a huge difference in the way people respond to you.

brilliant tip

Good eye contact tells the person you are aware, you care and you are in control.

This exercise should help if you need to improve your eye contact:

brilliant exercise

Ghost writer

(This technique works for a group of up to 20 people.)

The next time you're at a meeting, a party or social gathering, or presenting to a group, imagine you have an invisible colleague working with you ▶

(I know this sounds daft, but bear with me here). This person is sitting in the corner of the room watching your eye contact. Your colleague has a chart with the name of everyone present listed on it. Their job is simple: every time you look at someone while you're speaking, your colleague puts a tick against the person's name to record your eye contact. After the gathering, you sit down with your colleague to analyse the results. Ideally, they show that you gave each person in the room an equal share of your eye contact while you were talking.

There are a number of benefits to this exercise:

- You don't forget to look at people.
- You give each person an equal share of your attention.
- You don't stare at one person throughout (you may have been on the receiving end of this on occasions and wondered why the person speaking continually looked at you!).
- By looking at people, you engage them and send a clear message that you're interested in them.
- You look confident and in control.

You can't really use this technique for large groups of people. For larger audiences, try looking at them in small groups, picking one person out every now and then. Try to spread your focus across the whole audience so that no one feels left out.

Posture and stance

Some people just look confident. They don't need to do or change anything; they just have something about them. But why is this and what is that 'something'? More often than not it's to do with their posture. The way you hold yourself has a major impact on your body language and conveys your level of self-confidence. You don't need to say anything to look as though you lack confidence; poor body language can give it away on its own.

↗ brilliant exercise

Mirror image

You'll need a mirror for this exercise, preferably a full-size one so that you can see your whole body. You need to stand in front of it – but, before you do that, make a conscious effort to stand naturally, just as you normally would.

Now look at yourself. Ask yourself a simple question: 'Do I look confident?'
If you don't think so or you're not sure, try experimenting a little – try holding your head up, breathe in and push your chest out a little, keep your back straight and push your shoulders back.

Your aim is to look relaxed and yet aware and proud. I find that positioning one foot slightly in front of the other makes a difference, particularly when standing in front of or within a group. The alternative is to 'plant' yourself with both feet on the same line. This doesn't look so natural. Always make sure you have a small gap between your feet; you'll look rather stiff and tense otherwise. Try to distribute 40 per cent of your weight through your heels and 60 per cent throughout the ball of your foot and your toes. This brings your body position slightly forward and helps you to look more alert.

As long as you don't march up and down, there's nothing wrong with moving a little as you talk. It'll help you to look more relaxed. It should also help you to engage all members of the audience; moving your body (even just your upper body) to face people when you look at them, perhaps when asking or answering a question, helps to create a stronger link with them.

These simple changes in posture will help you to look and feel more sure of yourself.

They also help you to look more prominent. The reason for this is simple – having an open posture automatically takes up more space. It sends a physical message that you're not afraid. It also stops you looking defensive or shy.

Your walk

Have you ever thought about the way you walk? It seems like an odd question, doesn't it! It's worth thinking about though because, just like posture, it can have an impact on confidence. It's absolutely true that if you walk confidently, you'll feel more confident.

> if you walk confidently, you'll feel more confident

There are some simple things to consider to make this happen.

Don't walk too fast or too slowly; try to find the balance. Too fast could make you look in a panic or as though you're rushing, perhaps out of control. Too slowly could make you look de-motivated, disinterested, hesitant and could of course make you late! People with an air of confidence about them walk at a measured pace. So, reflect on the pace you walk at and try changing it if you need to. You'll need to think consciously about this; walking is such a natural action, we rarely think about how we do it. Try to incorporate the tips about posture while you're improving your walk – posture and walking should work together.

Your hands

Some people think that the best thing to do with your hands is to keep them by your side or hide them because otherwise they'll be a distraction. This is madness. It's akin to the soldier going into battle without using the ammunition on their belt.

Your hands should be an essential support to your verbal message. If used well, they can help you to reinforce your point. When in a relaxed environment, people tend to use their hands naturally to clarify and support their message. However, when in the spotlight, some people either completely forget about or lose control of their hands.

Don't fall into the trap of thinking that your hands will distract people. I very rarely meet people who are too demonstrative with their hand movements. The vast majority of people don't use their hands enough. The trick is to try to relax; let your hands do what comes naturally. The natural action is for them to move in support of your verbal message. This is why confident people look relaxed – their hands move naturally and in a coordinated way with their voice.

> confident people look relaxed – their hands move naturally

The following tips should help:

● Use your hands to emphasise or clarify your point. For example, if you plan to address a number of points, use your fingers to support this: hold up one finger when you're referring to point 1, two fingers for point 2 and so on. You could use two hands for this if you prefer – rest the fingers of one hand on the outstretched palm of the other. Another example might be when you're describing a minor issue – lift your hand so it can be seen, and bring your forefinger and thumb together to emphasise how small the issue is. There are of course many other examples that could be given. Try practising on your own using your hands to reinforce your verbal message. It can make a huge difference to people's perception of you.

● Have a 'default' or resting position for your hands when you're not using them. Otherwise, you'll look as though you don't know what to do with them. I find the most comfortable resting position to be arms slightly bent in front of your body, with your hands held together and fingers gently interlocked (without whites of knuckles showing!) You might prefer a different resting position so try experimenting and find your own – it's important that you're comfortable and relaxed with it, otherwise you won't use it.

● Use calm, smooth and flowing hand movements.

Here are some of the 'don'ts' to watch out for when using your hands:

● Don't use fast or jerky hand movements – they don't portray a confident demeanour and can be a distraction.

● Don't point at people.

● Don't fold your arms (unless in an informal environment where it doesn't matter). This could be seen as defensive and might make you appear unapproachable.

● Don't tap on surfaces with your fingers.

● Don't fidget, wring your hands or touch your face or neck. This can suggest you're feeling nervous or insecure; just as children often scratch their leg when telling a lie, adults scratch the back of their head, rub their arm or fiddle with their fingers when they're nervous.

● Don't forget that some hand signs can be deemed as inappropriate or rude in some cultures.

Facial expressions

Your facial expressions can convey a whole host of messages to people about your emotions, your feelings, your confidence levels and your interpretation of their message. Some people are naturally very expressive and open in their communication style. Others tend to be less expressive and 'private' and don't give much away at all. My experience is that confident people tend to fall mostly into the 'expressive' category although this is not always the case.

If, personally, you see yourself in the 'less expressive' category, try to think about how you could benefit by being slightly more expressive. For example, how often do you smile when talking to people? If the answer is 'not much' or 'never', you're missing a trick. If you really want to project confidence, try to smile more. A smile makes a huge difference. It makes you feel and look more confident and it makes the other person feel more at ease. A smile can send so many positive messages in an instant: happiness, awareness, interest, friendliness, approachability, sensitivity, enthusiasm and of course ... confidence.

> a smile can send so many positive messages in an instant

🔼 brilliant exercise

Guess who

Picture this – you're in a room with a group of people. You're either sitting round a table or standing. Any minute now, someone is going to open the door and come into the room. This person has 10 seconds to look at everyone in the room and guess who's in charge. Your aim is simple – to make sure the person picks you. There is one constraint only for the people in the room – *no one is allowed to talk.*

So, what are you going to do? The answer is simple because you haven't got much choice – you use your body language to win. You need to get your posture right, regardless of whether you're sitting or standing. In order to be picked, you'll need to look like the most alert and confident person in the room. If you're standing, the tips we've covered on your posture and stance will help.

To be picked as being in charge while you're sitting could be slightly more of a challenge because you only have the top half of your body to work with.

The temptation while you're sitting is to sit back, perhaps even slump in your chair. Try to resist this – you need to look aware, enthusiastic and interested the whole time.

▶

These actions should help:

- Sit leaning slightly forward in your chair.
- Keep your back straight, your shoulders back and your head up.
- Make sure you can see everyone and make regular eye contact with each person.
- Keep your hands above, not below the table (when you're not using them to support your message, rest them on the table).
- Use your facial expressions to help you to look alert and aware.
- Smile when appropriate.

Try this exercise the next time you're in a meeting or with a group of people in a room. It's a great way of helping yourself to look and feel more confident.

Space

You'll feel more confident if you feel comfortable with the 'space' around you. You probably know how uncomfortable you can feel if someone is too close to you during a conversation. Sometimes it's referred to as 'invading your personal space'. The perception and use of space differs significantly across cultures, so it's worth doing some research if you work or socialise within a culture with which you aren't familiar.

Don't make the mistake of thinking that to be confident is to be close enough so that you can control people's personal space. This is counter-productive because it just makes them feel uncomfortable. Ideally, you need to find the balance between proximity and distance.

Most of the time, you should be able to control the space around you. For example, you can make simple adjustments to where you position yourself to make sure you're not too close to people when you're in a group. Don't forget the 'Where?' element of the 'W' concept: if you have advanced warning, it's sensible to prepare the room if you're running a meeting or giving a presentation.

Space isn't just about the physical space around you though. It's also about your appearance. You'll feel more confident if you're happy with the way you look. Taking the time to do a little preparation can help here too. For example, if you know the dress code beforehand, you won't feel over- or under-dressed. There is one major rule here regardless – never look in a 'mess'. The word 'mess' doesn't only relate to your clothing, it also relates to your personal organisation and time management. If you look rushed, disorganised, ill-prepared or scatty, you're making life much more difficult for yourself if you want to feel confident.

Sometimes people don't realise how significant the messages you give out through bad use of space can be. For example, if at work your desk is always disorganised and in a mess, you send out negative messages. If you then, during the course of your work, need to be assertive and influential, you'll tend to be on the back foot. Your colleagues will see you as a 'messy person'; this could even have an impact on the respect they have for you. If this is the case, you're just making life more difficult for yourself.

brilliant tip

Take the initiative and control your personal space. Dress appropriately, keep tidy and use the space effectively.

First impressions

It takes just a very quick glance for someone to evaluate you and form a judgement when you meet them for the first time. Without even thinking consciously about it, the person forms an opinion about you. In literally just one second they're basing this on your body language, your appearance and your demeanour.

This first impression can be nearly impossible to reverse or undo. That's why it's *so* important to get it right. The last thing you want to be doing when you meet someone is to give away any sign that you lack confidence. Any negative impression you give will set the tone for the relation-

> a first impression can be nearly impossible to reverse or undo

ship that follows. So, regardless of whether it's in your work career or your social life, giving the best possible first impression is vital.

More often than not you'll have prior warning before you meet someone new. That means you'll have time to prepare. You don't need hours for this, you don't even need minutes – just a few seconds will do as long as you know how to make the most of the time you've got.

In short, your sole focus during that window of time before you shake the person's hand should be on looking confident. To do this you need to employ all the traits that constitute assertive behaviour. You should by now know what you need to work on here. Start this straight away the next time you meet someone new.

Remembering names

I don't know about you but I'm always impressed by people who remember names. These people always fall into the group of people I would describe as being confident. It's impressive if you meet someone and they then address you by your name; it's even more impressive if they do this when you're one of a group of people they've just met.

Remembering names is a simple concept that can really help you to stand out and be seen as a confident person. People seem to think it's much more difficult to do than it actually is; you'll have heard people say 'I'm hopeless at remembering names' – maybe you're one of these people yourself!

The main reason why people struggle to remember someone's name is that they don't register it in the first place. When you meet someone for the first time your senses are drawn mainly towards what they look like and how they behave. Without realising it, you get distracted from what they actually say. Of course, one of the first things they'll say is their name – and that's where the problem lies. You can't *forget* their name because you never actually *heard* it in the first place.

There are some simple steps you can take to get better at remembering names:

- *Prepare* – Get into the habit of accepting that an essential element of introducing yourself is hearing and remembering the person's name.

- *Ask* – If the person doesn't tell you their name, ask politely what it is.

- *Clarify* – If you don't hear the name clearly, politely ask them to tell you it again.

- *Associate* – Link the name with something physical that distinguishes the person.

- *Repeat* – Say the name to yourself until you remember it without thinking.

- *Write* – If it's a group, write their names down in the order they're sitting. Then test yourself with each person's name until you're comfortable you know them all 'off pat'.

- *Use* – Now that you've done the hard work of remembering the names, *use* them. Address people by their name regularly. They'll notice this, and their perception of you as a confident, aware and assertive person will build.

It's completely normal to feel a little anxious or nervous when you meet someone for the first time. Think consciously from now on about how you introduce yourself to people. By using positive verbal and non-verbal behaviour, you'll be able to give the very best first impression. The more you do this, the more confident and comfortable you'll feel when meeting people. When the other person sees that you are at ease, they too will feel more relaxed and the conversation is likely to flow much more easily.

CHAPTER 6

Handling conflict with confidence

There's an art to dealing confidently with conflict. Just as an army needs a strategy to win a battle, so, on a more tactical level, do *you* need tactics to deal with a personal skirmish. We all encounter these skirmishes from time to time, some of us even on a daily basis. But how do you normally react? You'll probably tend to react in the same way each time. That's because you have your own instinctive way of dealing with conflict.

> you have your own instinctive way of dealing with conflict

If you've started to use some of the tips covered so far in *Brilliant Confidence*, you should find that the number of conflict situations you encounter starts to reduce. For example, the simple act of adapting your communication style should make a huge difference to your relationships at work, at home and socially.

Your instinctive approach to conflict

Have you ever thought constructively about how you instinctively react when someone criticises you, says you're wrong, frustrates you or winds you up? Some people come out of their corner fighting every time, even when they think or even know the other person is right. Other people will just give in or avoid the conflict, even when they know the other person is wrong. What do you tend to do?

The conflict zone chart below shows two conflict handling extremes. Some people will 'contest' regardless of the situation; others will just 'give in'. Look at Figure 6.1 and put a cross on the line between 'contest' and 'give in' to show where you think your instinctive approach to conflict falls.

So you've drawn a cross somewhere on the line. Most people assess themselves correctly in terms of their leaning but some people find it difficult to judge the degree to which they lean; in other words, the strength of their style. To help with this, go to www.thinkconfidence.com and complete the Think Confidence Conflict Style Questionnaire. It's a simple questionnaire that helps you to identify your instinctive conflict style and the degree to which you use it.

Some people score themselves at one or the other extremes; others see themselves falling in the middle. This middle ground is the area of 'compromise'. You might think that to compromise is the right approach regardless of the situation – the solution that suits both people. Well that's true, but not *all* the time.

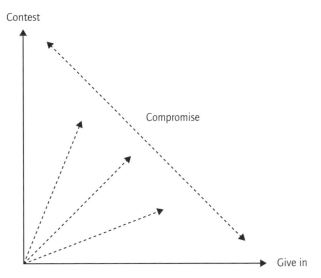

Figure 6.1 The conflict zone

You might also think that to be at one or the other extreme is wrong; after all, to 'give in' surely can't ever be right, can it? Well yes, in certain situations, it can. Equally, at the other extreme, some think that to 'contest' an issue strongly and to insist you're right could be construed as 'overdoing it'. Try not to think like this either – as long as you aren't aggressive or violent, contesting an issue can also be right in certain situations. The key is to have the self-discipline and confidence to choose the right approach for the right situation.

brilliant example

Jay

Jay was organising a weekend trip to France with a group of five friends. They'd arranged to meet in the local pub one evening. The aim was to discuss and agree where they would stay, how many nights they would stay for and what the travel arrangements would be. Everyone had agreed that Jay would be the best person to coordinate the trip because he had been to France the year before on a similar trip with other friends. Jay was happy to be in charge.

The meeting started off well. They were all good friends and had known each other for some time. There was, however, one person who was more outspoken than the rest and throughout the evening tended to dominate the conversation. Jay found this odd because during the course of the evening it transpired that this person (Lynda) had never even been to France before!

Jay remembered from his trip the year before that they'd really regretted not hiring a car for the weekend. They'd decided to go on the ferry as foot passengers and get the train to the village they were staying in. This had turned out to be a big mistake because, although beautiful and picturesque, the village was in the middle of nowhere. As a result, they'd ended up having to get taxis everywhere and this had meant they'd ended up spending much more than they'd planned. Not having a hire car had ▶

also meant they had no flexibility – every time they wanted to go out, they had to ring for a taxi. This had turned out to be really frustrating.

So, Jay explained all this when they were talking about transport arrangements. Lynda however just would not listen. She was adamant that the cost of taxis would be less than hiring cars. However, Jay had already worked out that, even if they hired two cars, it would still be cheaper than hiring taxis throughout the weekend and, of course, they'd have the flexibility to go where they wanted when they wanted.

This led to a disagreement. Jay began to feel very uncomfortable with the situation because he just didn't like arguing. He ended up giving in to Lynda even though he knew he was right. None of his other friends in the group could make up their minds what was best. One or two of them even tended to side with Lynda because she was so direct with her views. Jay just didn't stand up for himself so they weren't convinced by his argument – even though he'd actually been there and experienced the problem!

Jay just wasn't a person who felt comfortable contesting an issue. His instinct was to give in whenever he found himself in a conflict situation. He felt particularly uncomfortable with Lynda because she was a person who would instinctively contest.

The whole group lost out eventually because they didn't hire cars and, just as Jay had predicted, they regretted it.

---

brilliant tip

When you think you're right, don't give in. It's time to be actively assertive in order to contest the issue. You'll need to motivate yourself to do this, particularly if your instinct is to give in. Make a pact with yourself not to let this happen the next time you think you're right and the other person contests.

Like Jay, the majority of the people I meet who lack confidence tend to either give in or do their best to avoid the conflict in the hope that it will go away and not come back. The trouble is, the problem rarely does go away; more often than not it will fester and then come back with a vengeance.

So, you're probably getting a feel for what I'm suggesting here. People who have confidence and use this confidence in a balanced manner are able to deal with each conflict situation that confronts them in the way that best suits. They have the self-control and sensitivity to avoid or perhaps even give in when they should and they have the self-belief and self-confidence to stand up for themselves when they think they're right.

Identifying the type of conflict situation you're encountering is the first step to making a judgement and doing something about it. So, if any of the following applies, you need to dig deep, present your case confidently and *contest* the issue:

● When you're sure you're right and the potential repercussions of the other person winning the argument are serious.

● When you're sure you're right and any delay in presenting your case could have a negative impact.

On the other hand, when might it make sense to give in?

● When you know the person is right or has a better idea than you.

● When you know you are right but the issue is of such minor importance that it's just not worth getting into an argument.

● When you're working with someone who is learning (perhaps a young person) and you don't want to demotivate them. The person is full of energy and enthusiasm and wants to help. They come up with an idea that you know won't work because you perhaps tried it when *you* were learning. As long as the consequences of them trying their idea and failing aren't likely to be serious, let the person have a go. They'll feel more inclined to come up with ideas in the future because they know you'll listen. If you don't let them have a go, you could end up with a demotivated person who doesn't think you value their opinion or perhaps even trust them.

Or perhaps it would be more sensible to avoid the conflict (this isn't giving in; you're just avoiding the conflict for the moment with a view to addressing it again later if it's still there). So, when would it make sense to avoid it?

● When tempers are getting frayed and people aren't thinking straight.

● When the issue is of such minor importance that it's just a waste of time to argue about it.

● When you're not prepared properly with your argument.

● When you're not in the right frame of mind.

● When you're in a place that isn't appropriate (perhaps a public place where others can overhear you).

There are times too when the most sensible course of action is to compromise. If you score yourself between the two extremes on the conflict zone chart, your instinct will tend to push you towards the middle ground of compromise.

The compromise style lends itself best to the following situations:

● When a solution is moderately important but not worth the effort or possible continued conflict that might result from either contesting or giving in.

● When you need to achieve a temporary settlement to a larger issue.

● When you're under time pressure.

● When both sides have essential needs to consider.

● When you're dealing with someone of equal power or authority.

Choosing the right style

Be aware of your instinctive way of dealing with conflict; it could be to contest, to compromise or even to give in. Whichever it is, don't worry; there's nothing wrong with any of these approaches. Don't forget though – you'll react to conflict in your natural instinctive way time and time again if you don't consciously think about it. The key is to make sure you don't 'default' into your comfort zone when your instinctive approach isn't the *right* approach.

> don't 'default' into your comfort zone when your instinctive approach isn't the *right* approach

brilliant tip

Pinch yourself next time you face conflict. Look at how you're behaving. Ask yourself if you've chosen the right style.

Showing emotion

There's nothing wrong with showing your emotion! In fact, you'll find it hard to deal with conflict effectively if you withhold your true feelings. Some people might even perceive your lack of visible emotion as a sign that you don't care.

More often than not, the main reason we hold back is that we fear the consequences of showing our emotions. We worry that we'll embarrass ourselves and we wonder what the person will think of us and how they might react.

Try to set aside these worries. After all, there shouldn't be any embarrassment if you control the way you communicate your emotion. Continually holding in your emotion can be like blowing up a balloon – breath by breath it gets bigger until eventually, unless you release some of the air – BANG! Releasing *some* of the air is the important thing to remember here. If you let go of the balloon and release *all* of the air, it'll fly away wildly and you'll lose control. So, controlling the way you release the pressure is the key to communicating your emotion effectively.

These essential rules should stand you in good stead:

- Think carefully before you talk or act.
- Communicate your emotions in a controlled way.
- Don't let your emotions cloud your judgement.
- Make sure you're receptive to the emotions of the other person.
- Adapt your communication style to accommodate the style of the other person.

Dealing with difficult people

Even when you have the confidence to change the way you approach a conflict situation, from time to time you'll still encounter people who you find are difficult to deal with. Some of these people will be people you already know. That means you can pre-empt and prepare for what's going to happen before you see them; it's unlikely they're going to change the way they behave.

The first thing to do when dealing with a person you find difficult is to reflect on your natural communication style. Simply adapting your style to match theirs may well be enough to convert a 'difficult person' into a person you don't feel uncomfortable with. Hopefully you'll have nipped the problem in the bud before it's even started.

So, what should you do if you've tried adapting your style and still the person is being difficult and insisting they're right? Here are some ideas.

Stand up for yourself

I've mentioned that a lot of the people I meet who lack confidence find the hardest conflict situations to be the ones where they have to stand up for themselves. This may mean 'contesting' an issue, insisting on your rights or strongly voicing your concerns. They find this hardest because it's against their nature. If you're one of these people, you're going to find this one of the most challenging parts of your Confidence Project.

You'll find that being more assertive will help here. Think back to Chapter 5 – if you tend to lean naturally towards the passive side of the assertiveness seesaw, you'll have to work hard to fight your gremlin. Extreme passiveness normally means giving in. Your gremlin will be trying hard to keep you on the passive side of the bar. You'll never be able to stand up for yourself if you stay there. Remember the *Brilliant Confidence* principle – *don't let the gremlin get you.*

These three simple steps should also help when you need to stand up for yourself and when you encounter conflict:

Step 1 – Suss out the situation
Be quiet and don't rush in; control yourself and wait it out. Let the other person speak first – let them get it off their chest. Don't interrupt them. Actively listen, look alert and don't get distracted. Control your body language – don't let your body speak for you instead of your mouth. Don't fidget, shrug your shoulders or use submissive facial expressions. All these things are signs of conciliation and could make you look apologetic. Just stand or sit still, face the person and look them in the eye while they're talking.

Keep the person and the problem separate. No matter how much their behaviour frustrates you and winds you up, try to keep an open mind. The person might not just be being difficult; they might actually have a valid and good point.

keep the person and the problem separate

When they've finished, try to hold the silence. This might put them off their guard. They're expecting you to say something – so you've got the initiative now. Make sure that when your chance to respond comes, you insist that nobody interrupts you. This shouldn't be a problem if you had the self-control not to interrupt *them*. If you're interrupted, politely remind the person that you deserve to be heard – it's your turn now.

Step 2 – Deliver

Make sure you know what you want to achieve and the basis of your argument. If you don't, you're not ready – so find more time to prepare. If *you* don't know, how can the other person be expected to understand your point of view?

Take control by setting out the facts. There's no harm in repeating the other person's argument or position back to them. This way they'll know you've listened. Having heard it again, they might even realise how stupid or weak it sounds! Repeating it back to them also gives you more chance to think about it.

take control by setting out the facts

Then, speak authoritatively in the first person. This means saying 'I' more than you might normally. For example, it's more constructive to say 'I don't agree with you' than 'You're wrong'. There's nothing wrong with saying 'I disagree' or 'I feel strongly that that is the wrong approach', etc. Make sure you have some substance to back up your opinion though. Otherwise the other person could counter that you're basing your opinion simply on judgement, not fact. This could also mean that you start to lose credibility – and then you're on the slippery slope to losing the argument.

There's one exception to the principle of saying 'I' – never say 'I'm sorry' for your opinion. Never apologise for standing up for yourself unless, on reflection, your behaviour was aggressive or inappropriate in some way.

Speak assertively; try not to stutter and don't mumble. Remember to breathe! This will help you to think and speak at a measured pace. Be positive at all times and don't be frightened to encourage discussion about the issue. Even though the person might eventually realise you're right, they won't necessarily accept this if they don't feel you've given them a chance to present their thoughts in full.

Step 3 – Take the initiative at the end

Take control of the conflict situation by being the one to conclude it. Have the moral courage to offer an ultimatum if you think it's warranted. Try to end it on your terms but be prepared to compromise if you judge it to be fair and necessary. If you've decided to contest the issue, never walk away without either solving it or agreeing a next step.

---

brilliant example

Naomi

Naomi was rather like Jay in her approach to conflict. Her instinct was to give in rather than hurt someone's feelings or, even better, to avoid the conflict altogether in the hope that it would go away.

The trouble was, she'd tried both these approaches and still she kept coming into conflict with a particular person (Marie). They were both

▶

managers of a call centre team dealing with holiday insurance. They worked different shifts and as a result didn't see much of each other.

Naomi had got to the point where she felt the team was suffering due to Marie's insistence on shaping the way it operated. Naomi would regularly come in to work and find that Marie had introduced a new procedure that she knew nothing about. Not only did Naomi feel this was unprofessional, because they were supposed to be managing the team jointly, she also felt that some of these new procedures were wrong and inefficient.

Naomi decided to try out the three-step plan to deal with Marie. She had to summon up a significant amount of courage to do this because it meant going completely against her instinct. The first thing she did was arrange a meeting with Marie. She explained beforehand that the reason for the meeting was to talk about the most recent new procedure Marie had introduced.

Step 1 was easy for Naomi – all she had to do was look Marie in the eye, listen and take in exactly what she said. She didn't even have to invite Marie to speak because Marie immediately launched into justifying why she'd introduced the new procedure. Naomi also made a point of taking some notes while Marie was speaking. They were just far enough away from each other so that Marie couldn't read them. Naomi noticed her looking down at them every now and then. This made her feel more confident; she was sure she detected a sense of unease in Marie's behaviour.

Step 2 was harder – Naomi had to deliver her points. This was against her natural inclinations. She waited until Marie had finished. She finished the note she was taking and looked up. She let the silence extend. Just as she sensed Marie was about to start talking again, she spoke up. She started by summarising what Marie had said (her notes were helpful here). She explained clearly why she felt the procedure wasn't working and suggested another solution. At one point Marie tried to interrupt. Naomi said very assertively, 'I've listened carefully to your points – I would like to finish explaining mine please'. Marie stopped talking immediately.

Naomi didn't let Marie interrupt until she'd finished. They then had a discussion. Naomi was clear in her mind right from the start that she wouldn't give in. She'd thoroughly researched her argument and was prepared to stand up for it. She was surprised to see that after a while, Marie backed down and believe it or not *accepted* it.

Step 3 went well too – Naomi kept the initiative by explaining she didn't feel it was in the best interests of the team for Marie to make decisions without involving her. She proposed that from now on they meet once a week so that they could manage the team more effectively together. Marie seemed a little wary of this idea but agreed to it in the interests of the team.

Naomi found that subsequently, over time, her working relationship with Marie improved. It was never fantastic but the change in her approach to dealing with the conflict with Marie made a huge difference. Marie started to get used to this and in time even admitted privately that she respected Naomi more for it and found it easier to work with her because she 'knew where she stood with her'.

The following tips should also help you to stop conflict escalating when you encounter it:

- Ask yourself whether it really matters that much – in other words, is it worth getting into an argument? What's the worst-case scenario?
- Change the subject – stop talking about it.
- Don't repeat the argument to others to make you feel better or just to get it off your chest.
- Put yourself in the other person's shoes – see it from their side.
- Choose not to associate with negative people or people who argue for argument's sake.
- Focus on fact, not emotion.
- Clear your mind. Get out of the environment, go for a walk or do some physical exercise.

- Compliment the person. Some people are very susceptible; you might find that just being nice can help you to win the argument or get your way.

- Acknowledge that you've heard the other person's point of view. Some people just need to know that you are listening and you understand their concerns.

- Use open-ended, not closed questions. An open-ended question invites discussion, a closed question invites a 'Yes' or 'No' answer. For example:

    - Open ended question: 'How did you think that meeting went?'

    - Closed question: 'Did you think that meeting went well?'

- Manage the person's expectations; don't promise you can do everything. If you say you'll do something, make sure you can and will do it. You'll gain more respect and people will know where they stand with you.

- Don't send emotionally charged or angry emails. Try to deal with the issue face to face. If you have no choice and must reply to someone by email, try writing the email first but don't send it. Have a break and cool down, then have another look at it. Don't send it until you make sure it is written in a controlled and professional way. It could backfire on you otherwise.

Have no fear!

There should be no need for you to fear conflict from now on. You'll feel more confident to deal with it if you try to see disagreement as something that's bound to happen from time to time – you can't stop it happening but you *can* deal with it. Approach it as a natural phenomenon that's part of life. It's a fact that people behave and think differently and therefore, on occasions, they'll disagree with each other.

That's actually a good and positive thing – if we were all the same, we would progress as a race of people at a much slower rate. It's proven for instance that the most successful teams are the ones with the most diverse mix of personalities, knowledge and intelligence. The key to real success is understanding how to turn any differences of opinion (conflict) into agreement and effective action.

If you really think about it and try to analyse why conflict occurs, more often than not you'll come to the conclusion that it stems from differences in personal style and approach. A disagreement may start as a result of differences in opinion but the escalation to conflict often comes as a result of differences in behaviour. In extreme cases the differences in opinion are completely forgotten and the clashes in style and behaviour take over as the core conflict issue itself.

brilliant tip

Expect disagreements to happen. Your challenge is to deal calmly with each situation so that it doesn't escalate into conflict. Remember the three key steps: wait, deliver, take the initiative.

CHAPTER 7

Embracing the change

'You gain strength, experience and confidence through every experience where you really stop to look fear in the face. You must do the thing you cannot do.'

Eleanor Roosevelt, American First Lady and humanitarian

Doing the thing you cannot do means *making a change*.

You've probably already realised that putting your Confidence Project into action is going to mean making some changes in the way you think and behave. You may have made some changes already. You may even have done some things you previously *could not do*. If so, brilliant! You haven't let the thought of doing something different hinder you.

Some people do find the concept of change harder to deal with than others. Don't worry if you're one of these people; no one finds it easy. There's a simple reason for this. Human nature instils within us a natural and instinctive caution whenever we're faced with doing something new or different. This of course is a positive trait; it stops us rushing into things that are ill-conceived, foolish or even dangerous.

People with self-confidence are able to control this natural caution. They understand why it's there but they have the self-confidence and self-belief to make sure it doesn't work

people with self-confidence are able to control their natural caution

against them or hold them back when they need to change their behaviour or when an opportunity arises.

So how do you find the right balance between caution and action? In other words, how can you help yourself to get moving with the changes *you* have decided to make as part of your Confidence Project? To do this, you need to understand what happens in your mind when you're faced with the need to change.

Dealing with change within your Confidence Project

You may well be wondering what I actually mean by 'change'. In terms of your Confidence Project, 'change' means doing any of the following *differently* to the way you normally do it:

● *Communicating verbally* – For example, one of the changes you may have decided to make in your Confidence Project is to speak louder or perhaps more slowly in certain situations.

● *Communicating non-verbally* – You may have identified that you need to look people in the eye more when you're talking to them or perhaps you need to change your posture.

● *Thinking* – Perhaps you've realised that you tend to be too negative and that you need to think more positively from now on.

● *Behaving* – You may have realised that your present lifestyle isn't conducive to being more confident. For example, you may have decided that you need to get a grip of yourself, be more organised and more focused.

These are just a few examples of changes people decide to make. The changes *you* need to make for your Confidence Project to be successful may be similar or perhaps very different. You'll have got a good feel for these during the perception exercises in Chapter 3.

A natural reaction

It's natural for you to feel more safe and secure if you carry on doing what you used to do rather than try out something new. This is because we tend to prefer to do what we know works, even if it doesn't work very well! This may also be true of your approach to 'change' in relation to your Confidence Project; you'll probably feel uncomfortable moving out of your comfort zone (the way you used to be) because it is 'safer' to stay as you are.

we tend to prefer to do what we know works

The critical point to have at the forefront of your mind though is that through *Brilliant Confidence*, you've made some rational decisions; you've decided that certain things *aren't* working for you. These are the things that are hindering your confidence levels, self-belief and possibly even self-esteem too. Therefore, they *must change* if you want your Confidence Project to succeed.

Try to keep this in proportion though. For a lot of the time, there's no problem with staying as you are. It's just in certain situations and with certain people that you need to change the way you communicate and behave.

The change process

Coming to terms with the need to make these changes involves your mind going through a number of stages (don't worry, I'm not going to boggle you with some complicated psychological theory here). It's true though that we all go through the same thought processes when dealing with change. In simple terms, there are two stages to this:

● *Stage 1* – Coming to terms with and accepting the need to change.

● *Stage 2* – Putting the change into practice.

Although we all go through these two stages, some people move more quickly than others. That's simply because, depending on their personality, some people accept and embrace change more willingly than others. There's a difference of course between thinking of and initiating the change *yourself* and being told or invited to change by *someone else*. Most people find the latter more challenging; not only do you have to make the change, you also have to come to terms with the other person's reasoning. In the main, your Confidence Project involves the former which, you'll be glad to hear, tends to be easier; *you* are the initiator of the change and, therefore, it's yourself you need to reason with and convince of the need. This surely shouldn't be a problem – should it?

Hopefully, you're already well into this process. Ideally, you will already have come to terms with and accepted the need to change. What you've read so far in *Brilliant Confidence* should certainly have whetted your appetite. Let's not make any assumptions though – as I said, some people move through the process more quickly than others, so it's helpful to look at what's going on in your mind in a little more detail.

> some people move through the process more quickly than others

Stage 1 – Coming to terms with and accepting the need to change

Denial

To succeed at your Confidence Project and change for the better, you'll need to break some pretty strong moulds. Regardless of whether you initiate the change yourself or someone else suggests it, the very first thought that comes into our minds when the need for change is introduced is *denial*. We deny the need for it and don't want to do it. For some people, this is just a momentary thought, for others it dwells and then festers. In the worst case, it can be so destructive that it actually stops any possibility of the change taking place.

Without wanting to frighten you, unless you can control it, denial could be responsible for bringing your Confidence Project to a grinding halt before it's even properly started.

Resistance

But don't worry, the fact that you started reading *Brilliant Confidence* in the first place suggests that you're already well past the denial stage in terms of accepting the need and wanting to be a more confident person. If so, you've moved on to the next step of the change process – resistance.

Resistance involves a passive acceptance that you need to do some things differently. Whereas before, in denial, the door of your Confidence Project may have been firmly shut and locked, now, at the resistance stage, you have the key in your hand. You still need to put it in the lock and open the door though. Here are some of the reasons why people struggle to use the key – in other words, why people find it hard to overcome this passive resistance to making a change.

Can you remember ever experiencing thoughts like these? (you'd be unusual if you can't):

● You fear doing it.

● You fear the result of it.

● You can't be bothered to do it.

● You haven't got the time to do it.

● You're scared of taking a step into the unknown.

● You see the need to change as a criticism of you.

● You fear the embarrassment of doing it or being seen doing it.

● You fear the possibility of failure.

You know yourself better than anyone. In order to get your Confidence Project off to the best possible start and to keep it moving, it's essential that you know where you stand here. In other words, how willingly do you embrace change? This exercise should help you to work it out.

⤢ brilliant exercise

Think change

Try to think back to times in the past when you've had to make changes. Think of your life as a whole. To help you, here are some examples of changes other people remember in their lives: giving up smoking, getting fit, changing jobs, redecorating the house, being more sociable, etc. These are just some examples, none of which may be relevant to you – but which changes can *you* remember?

Once you've recalled them, think carefully about how you approached them. Try to think right back to the very beginning of each experience. Try to remember how you felt when you first thought about making the change. How long did it take you to come to terms with it? Do you remember denying initially and then resisting the need for it? If so, did you have the self-confidence to overcome this denial and resistance yourself or did someone else have to help you?

If someone else had to help you, you're not alone; you're one of many people I meet who struggle right at the very beginning at the denial stage. You now know from this experience that you'll have to work extra hard at the beginning of your Confidence Project to get it moving. Some people find it helpful to work with a 'buddy' at this stage of the project. So, if you think you might need some help to get motivated at the start, think of someone (a buddy) who could support you and work with you on it. If you worked with someone during the 'Straight talking' perception exercise in Chapter 3, maybe the same person could help you and give you some moral support here.

On the other hand, like some people, you might not want any help. That's fine too. After all, your Confidence Project is something personal, something you may well want to keep to yourself. Don't worry if you're thinking like this – as they say 'fore-warned is fore-armed'. The important thing is that you know from reflecting back on your reaction to change in the past that you're vulnerable to denial and resistance; so now you're in a stronger position to deal with that weakness yourself (see Figure 7.1).

But deal with it you *must*.

brilliant tip

A word of warning: don't allow your Confidence Project to stall before it's really started. Smother your gremlin if it tries to tempt you into denial or resistance. Try asking yourself what the alternative is to making the change; what will the consequences be if you don't change? This alone should be enough to convince you of the need.

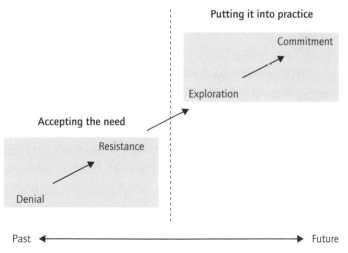

Figure 7.1 Dealing with change during your Confidence Project

Stage 2 – Putting the change into practice

Exploration

When you reach the 'exploration' stage in your state of mind, you'll have accepted the need to change and you'll be exploring new ways of behaving and communicating. You're looking to the future, not dwelling on the past. You might think you've reached exploration already – if so, that's great! The fact that you're reading *Brilliant Confidence* certainly suggests this because you're using the book to *explore* ways of building your confidence.

> you're looking to the future, not dwelling on the past

Don't worry if you feel you're not quite there yet though – it's normal to move back and forth between resistance and exploration for a little while. It's entirely understandable that you're a little anxious about some of the things you're going to need to do to get your Confidence Project really moving.

So, it's important to work out where you personally are in your mindset right now. If you want to change but your gremlin is still getting in the way and nibbling away at you, you've got a little bit more work to do to silence it. You'll need self-discipline for this.

You'll know when you've truly reached the exploration stage. It will be like waking up to a new dawn. Denial and resistance can be like experiencing a tempestuous storm at sea; exploration is like waking up the next morning to find clear blue skies and calm all around. You can see clearly out ahead, right to the distant horizon. You now need to set your course; without that you're in danger of drifting, going round in circles or potentially even heading back the way you came. You can't let that happen.

During exploration you're getting your bearings and working out a plan of action. You're clarifying your vision of what you want your new future to look like. You're thinking positively about the real changes you need to make in your life to feel more confident. You're starting to think in terms of the benefits of doing these things rather than how hard they will be to do. You'll probably still feel anxious about doing some of them but the difference is that, whereas before you weren't convinced it was possible to feel and be more confident, now you're starting to believe it really is.

If I were to guess where you are now in your mindset, I would say you're probably on the cusp between exploration and commitment.

Commitment

Exploration will lead naturally to 'commitment' as long as you stay positive in your mindset. Commitment is the last stage of the change process. You've set aside any negative thoughts, you've come to terms with what's ahead and you can see the benefits of committing yourself to your Confidence Project.

You've reached the point where you're ready to launch the project. You've accepted the challenge and decided that the effort will be worth it. You feel *committed* to making the project work. In short – you're all systems *go*!

Don't get too carried away though. It's great to be committed but dangerous if you bite off more than you can chew to start with. It's important to manage your expectations and take one step at a time. The objective and goal-setting principles in Chapter 2 should help you here. Start slowly with small changes so that you don't frighten yourself off. While you're doing this, try to set specific milestones to mark your progress.

manage your expectations and take one step at a time

True commitment comes with time. It helps if, step by step, you can actually see positive results from your efforts. Slowly but surely your self-confidence will build and your commitment to try new ways of behaving will strengthen.

brilliant tip

People go at different speeds through the change process. It's OK to go slowly as long as you keep moving and don't get stuck. It's also OK to go fast, as long as you truly commit to the change at the end. Don't kid yourself. Commitment means actually doing things differently, breaking some habits and putting yourself in situations that perhaps terrified you previously.

The artist Vincent Van Gogh once said:

'If you hear a voice within you say "you cannot paint", then by all means paint, and that voice will be silenced.'

He may well have been referring to his gremlin.

Conclusion: Making it happen

You've probably been trying out some of the exercises and tips you've read in *Brilliant Confidence*. That's great; that's exactly what you should have been doing. The road map in Chapter 1 steered you in that direction and encouraged you to do it. That means you've well and truly started your Confidence Project.

Now think back to where we began. You'll remember Sid, my neighbour: brick by brick he built his house. He started by clearing the ground, laying the foundations and setting the cornerstones. Having read *Brilliant Confidence*, you're now at this point in *your* building programme.

You've cleared away the past, built a firm foundation and you've cast four key cornerstones:

- positive mental attitude
- focus – personal objectives and goals
- communication style – assertiveness and influence
- embracing change.

These cornerstones form the heart and lifeblood of your Confidence Project. They're the mainstays to building your confidence from now on; keep them at the forefront of your mind.

It took my neighbour 18 months before he could stand proudly in front of what he'd built. It's impossible to say how long it's going to take you; everyone's different. Some people's

Confidence Project takes a matter of weeks, others take months, others perhaps even years.

Keep your expectations realistic. Start by setting yourself small, manageable challenges. Don't get disappointed if some things don't work out as you hoped or planned. That's bound to happen on occasions. Keep trying regardless. Treat every experience as a learning experience no matter what happens. Make sure you do learn from it though, so that next time you do it better.

start by setting yourself small, manageable challenges

At some point, you'll start to feel that you're there; you've finished your project. You'll have the self-confidence to describe yourself as a confident person! Great, *well done*! But stay aware, don't let yourself get complacent. Your confidence levels will ebb and flow. It happens to us all; it's natural. Even the most confident people take a knock every now and then. The key is to reflect and to look positively at the experience, learn from it and move on; you have all the tools to do this now.

You've read *Brilliant Confidence* so you'll always have this knowledge base – your job now is to *build* on it. Don't leave the cornerstones untouched without giving them something to support. Otherwise, over time, they'll become overgrown and covered with brambles and weed. They're no good to you then; they're wasted. You built them, *now build on them*.

Just as the house was built with bricks, your Confidence Project will be built with *practice*. Practice requires you to have the self-discipline to put yourself in situations out of your comfort zone; situations from which you would previously have shied away. The more you practise, the stronger you will feel and the more confident you will become.

the more you practise, the stronger you will feel and the more confident you will become

Sometimes you'll have to curb your natural instincts; you'll have to behave differently to the way you normally behave; you'll have to adapt your style. You could even say you'll have to 'act' the right 'part' for the right situation. There's nothing wrong with that at all. It doesn't mean you're being 'false', it means you're being *clever.*

Planning for action

To keep the momentum moving from this point on, you need a plan. The best way to do this is to plan your project on a weekly and then daily basis.

Weekly plan

At the start of each week, look ahead at the whole week and identify the events that require you to be confident. These will be social and work related. They'll be situations like meeting new people at a social engagement; speaking assertively when you take back an item to a shop; contributing more positively in a meeting at work; going to the doctor or dentist; telling a neighbour about something you're unhappy with; giving a presentation at work ... the list is endless. Once you know what's coming up, you've already started to think and prepare mentally for it.

Fight your gremlin when it tries to convince you that these events are nightmares waiting to happen. We all have these feelings on occasions – even confident people. They won't let the gremlin get to them though. You mustn't either.

Use your initiative. Don't just think reactively about the week ahead. In other words, don't only focus on the events that *others* have requested you to attend and the jobs *they've* asked you to do. Think also of opportunities *you* can present yourself with. These may well be the opportunities that you would previously have dismissed outright or avoided, even though, deep down, you knew you should have seized them. Winston Churchill put his finger on it when he famously quoted: 'The optimist sees opportunity in every danger; the pessimist sees danger in every opportunity.'

So, for example: have the courage to put yourself forward when your boss needs a volunteer to do a presentation; take a positive step when there's an opportunity to make new friends; and seize the chance when you have an opportunity to learn something new. Tell yourself that no longer will you let opportunities in life pass you by. If *you* don't take them, somebody else, someone *more confident* than you, probably will. That's just not right. It's daft, it makes no sense. You can't let it happen any more.

> no longer will you let opportunities in life pass you by

Daily plan

At the beginning of each day, you'll need to psyche yourself up. Just like a professional sports person prepares mentally for a match, so *you* should prepare for each day of your Confidence Project. You'll need to be strict about this at the beginning, otherwise you'll forget. After a while, you'll get into the habit of thinking positively about the day ahead.

When you're trying something new (for example, one of the tips you've read in *Brilliant Confidence*), aim to do it for 21 days. Twenty-one days is the magical period of time for which you need to do something before it becomes a regular habit. Bear this in mind and try it; it really works.

Start as you mean to go on. Set aside a little time, just a few minutes, at the beginning of each day. Think about the day ahead: play out in your mind each situation you're likely to be confronted with and the people involved. Of course, there will be some situations you can't foresee; there's no way of knowing they're going to happen. That's to be expected. The key is that the better you get at dealing with the situations you *can* foresee, the more confident you'll feel when dealing with those you can't.

Minute by minute

Stay alert at all times. Your gremlin could ambush you at any time – probably when you're least expecting it. Remember, your gremlin prefers you as you *used to be* and will be trying to hold you back. Only a positive and focused mindset will keep it at bay.

No longer are you on your own; you have your Confidence Project to support you now. Have it at the forefront of your mind at all times. Push out the boundaries, have the courage to behave differently. Keep practising, keep learning and slowly but surely your confidence will grow.

Don't rush. Never panic. Take one step at a time.

Good luck on your journey!

'Self-confidence is the first requisite to great undertakings.'

Samuel Johnson, English writer and critic

Index